BIG ENGLISH

3

2ND EDITION
STUDENT'S BOOK
with online resources

Contents

Unit	Vocabulary	Structures
Welcome to Class! pp. a–d	**Rooms:** bathroom, bedroom, kitchen, living room **Furniture:** couch, dresser, table, sink **Clock times:** eight o'clock, nine o'clock, seven o'clock, ten o'clock **Activities:** brush my teeth, do my homework, eat lunch, get up, go to bed, school starts, watch TV	I always get up early on school days. I usually eat breakfast with my family.
1 Wake Up! pp. 4–15	**Daily routines:** brush my teeth, do my homework, eat breakfast, feed the cat, get dressed, play soccer, play video games, wake up, wash my face, watch TV **Times:** seven o'clock, seven ten, seven thirty, seven forty-five	What does he do before/after school? He eats breakfast before/after school.
2 A Lot of Jobs! pp. 16–27	**Jobs:** cashier, chef, farmer, firefighter, mail carrier, nurse, police officer, scientist, teacher, waiter **Places:** farm, fire station, hospital, laboratory, police station, restaurant, store, school	What does she do? She's a firefighter. Where does he work? He works at a fire station. What do your sisters do? They're chefs.
3 Working Hard! pp. 28–39	**Chores:** clean my room, do the dishes, feed the fish, make my bed, practice the piano, study for a test, take out the trash, walk the dog **Adverbs of frequency:** always, never, usually, sometimes	What does she have to do? She has to feed the fish. What do you have to do? I have to clean my room. We always/usually/sometimes/never take out the trash.

Checkpoint Units 1–3 pp. 40–43

Unit	Vocabulary	Structures
4 Amazing Animals pp. 44–55	**Animals:** bear, camel, deer, lizard, owl, penguin, sea lion, shark, toucan **Habitats:** desert, forest, ice and snow, jungle, lake, mountain, ocean, rain forest	What can a bear do? It can swim. It can't fly. What can owls do? They can fly. They can't climb. Can a penguin jump? Yes, it can./No, it can't. Can lizards swim? Yes, they can./No, they can't.
5 Wonderful Weather! pp. 56–67	**Weather:** cloudy, cold, cool, hot, rainy, snowy, sunny, warm, windy **Clothes:** boots, coat, gloves, hat, raincoat, sandals, scarf, shorts, sunglasses, sweater, umbrella **Times:** today, yesterday	What's the weather like today? It's hot and sunny. What was the weather like yesterday? It was windy. Leaves were everywhere.
6 Smells Good! pp. 68–79	**Verb senses:** feels, looks, sounds, smells, tastes **Adjectives:** awful, bad, beautiful, delicious, good, horrible, nice, soft, sweet, terrible, tight	How does the apple pie taste? It tastes delicious. How do your new shoes feel? They feel tight.

Checkpoint Units 4–6 pp. 80–83

Unit	Vocabulary	Structures
7 Fabulous Food! pp. 84–95	**Food:** bread, cucumber, green peppers, lettuce, mushrooms, mustard, olives, onions, pizza, sandwich, tomato sauce, turkey	Is there any pizza? Yes, there is some pizza./No, there isn't any pizza. Are there any sandwiches? Yes, there are some sandwiches./No, there aren't any sandwiches.
8 Healthy Living pp. 96–107	**Healthy living:** eat/have breakfast, eat/have a healthy lunch, drink water, get any exercise, get enough sleep, ride a bike	Did you get enough sleep yesterday? Yes, I did./No, I didn't.
9 School Trips! pp. 108–119	**Places:** aquarium, art gallery, concert hall, dairy farm, national park, museum, theater, zoo **Verbs:** heard, learned, liked, looked, saw, went	Where did you go? I went to an art gallery. What did she see? She saw a play. Did they like it? Yes, they liked it./No, they didn't like it.

Checkpoint Units 7–9 pp. 120–123

Cambridge Young Learners English: Movers Practice Paper pp. 124–132   **Cutouts** pp. 133–138

CLIL: Content and Culture	Writing	Phonics	Values	I can...
Life Science: Keeping clean bacteria, cough, decay, germs, healthy, sick, sneeze **Around the World: Time zones** different, map, time zone	Sentence: Subjects and Verbs	a_e, i_e, o_e cake, face, game, shape bike, like, time, ride bone, home, note	Do your chores.	...use words for daily activities. ...use *before* and *after* to talk about when things happen. ...talk about what I do every day. ...write sentences with subjects and verbs.
Social Science: Creative jobs create, drawings, galleries, materials, paintings, photo shoot, professional, work of art **Around the World: Communities** be proud of, collect, community, contest, donate, get lost, trash	Sentence: Compound Subjects and Verbs	sm, st, sp, sk smart, smile, smoke star, stop, storm space, Spain, spoon skates, ski, skin	Respect others.	...use job words. ...use *what* and *where* to ask and answer about what people do and where they work. ...talk about what people do and where they work. ...write sentences with compound subjects or verbs.
Math: Pocket money adult, cash, cost, earn, let (someone) know, save, stranger **Around the World: Work** bucket, fire, forest, handle, lamp, oil, pump, stove, wind, wood	Paragraph: Titles	ay, oy day, May, pay, ray, say, way boy, joy, soy, toy	Always be happy to help.	...use words for chores and other kinds of work. ...use *have to* to talk about how often people do things. ...use *always*, *usually*, *sometimes*, and *never* to talk about chores. ...use capital letters in titles.
Life Science: Camouflage blend in, bottom of the ocean, hunt, stone, tree bark **Around the World: Pets** alligators, canaries, geckos, goldfish, parakeets, snakes, tarantulas	Paragraph: Topic Sentences	ea, oi, oe bean, eat, meat peach, sea, tea boil, coin, oil foe, toe	Protect animals and their habitats.	...use words for animals and where they live. ...use *can* to ask and answer questions about what animals can do. ...talk about what animals can do and where they live. ...write topic sentences.
Geography: Climate average, climate, degrees Celsius, desert, dry, extreme, mild, minus **Around the World: Weather** average, hot springs, rain forest, rink, sand dunes, temperatures, tropical	Paragraph: Detail Sentences	sc, sw, sn, sl scar, scarf, scout swan, sweet, swim snack, snail, snow sleep, slim, slow	Prepare for the weather.	...use words for the weather and what clothes people wear in different types of weather. ...use *is* and *was* to ask and answer about the weather today and yesterday. ...talk about the weather around the world and what people wear. ...write detail sentences.
Life Science: Animal senses avoid, brain, danger, echo, information, senses, sound waves, taste buds, tongue **Around the World: Jobs** awful, clean, fresh, smelly, stink, take care of, wet	Paragraph: Final Sentences	fl, pl, gl, bl flag, flip-flops, fly plant, play, plum glad, glass, glow black, block, blow	Try new things.	...use words for how things look, feel, taste, smell, or sound. ...use verbs and adjectives to talk about the five senses. ...talk about the five senses. ...write final sentences.
Science: Vitamins blood, bone, brain, energy, healthy, iron, muscle, skin, teeth, vitamin **Around the World: Global food** bake, boil, dough, fry, oil, pickled, soup, spicy, steam	Paragraphs	br, cr, dr, fr, gr, pr, tr bread, brick cream, cry dream, drive frog, from grass, green train, troll	Try different foods.	...use food words. ...use *some* and *any* to ask and answer questions about food. ...ask and answer about food. ...write a paragraph about my favorite meal.
Science: Keeping healthy active, activities, body, burn, calorie, measure, put on weight **Around the World: Strange sports** contest, net, puck, race, regatta, team	Combining sentences with *and*, *but*, *or*	all, au, aw all, ball, call, tall, wall haul, Paul claw, draw, law, yawn	Get exercise.	...use words for healthy and unhealthy habits. ...use *did* and *didn't* to ask and answer questions about healthy and unhealthy habits. ...ask and answer about healthy and unhealthy habits. ...combine sentences with *and*, *but*, and *or*.
Art: Paintings artist, colorful, happy, impressionist, painter, sad, strange **Around the World: Stage performances** dramatic, flamenco, open-air theater, performance, play, popular, puppet, show, stage	Sentence: subjects, verbs, and objects	nt, ld, nd, st ant, plant, tent child, cold, old band, hand, sand chest, fast, nest	Recognize your talents.	...use words for places to visit on a school trip. ...ask and answer questions using the past simple. ...talk about school trips. ...write sentences with a subject, verb, and object.

Welcome to Class!

1 Listen and read. What does Luke's uncle do?

a Welcome Unit

Welcome to Class!

2 Look at the story. Circle T for true or F for false.

1 Luke's uncle goes to bed at 3:00.   T   F
2 Luke's uncle eats breakfast at 9:00.   T   F
3 Luke's uncle watches TV at 6:00.   T   F
4 Luke's uncle gets up at 11:00.   T   F

3 Read and write.

> couch   dresser   sink   table

1 The _____ is in the kitchen.
2 The _____ is in the living room.
3 The _____ is in the bathroom.
4 The _____ is in the bedroom.

4 Look and write do or does. Then answer the question.

1 What time _____ Luke's uncle usually get up?
   At _____

2 What time _____ Luke's uncle usually eat breakfast?
   At _____

3 What time _____ Luke and his uncle go to bed on Saturday?
   At _____

4 What time _____ Luke's uncle usually watch TV?
   At _____

5 What time _____ Luke and his uncle get up on Sunday?
   At _____

Welcome Unit   b

Welcome to Class!

 Listen and number in order.

a brush teeth   b eat lunch

c go to bed   d school start   e get up

f watch TV   g do homework

6 **Listen again. Draw the times.**

7 **Work with a partner. Ask and answer.**

 When do you brush your teeth?

I brush my teeth at 7 o'clock.

c Welcome Unit

Welcome to Class!

8 Listen and number in order. Then say.

a
I always get up early on school days.

b
I usually eat breakfast with my family.

c
I usually get my backpack ready the night before school.

d
I always go to school at 8:00.

9 Write about you.

1 I usually get up at _____ .
2 I have breakfast at _____ .
3 I usually watch TV at _____ .
4 I go to bed at _____ .

10 Play the game.

Welcome Unit   d

1 Wake Up!

Vocabulary

I will learn to name daily routines and times.

🎵 Song Time! 🎵

1 Listen, look, and say.
Monday, May 13

1 wake up

2 wash my face

3 eat breakfast

4 get dressed

5 brush my teeth

6 play soccer

7 play video games

8 do my homework

9 feed the cat

10 watch TV

2 Play the time game.

4 Unit 1

Song

I will learn to ask and answer about daily routines and times.

3 Listen and sing. What does Kate do?

Hurry, Kate!

It's Monday, 7:30.
Kate has to wake up.
Her mom sees the clock and says
Wake up, sleepy head.

Kate has her backpack
And she has her lunch.
What time is it now?
Oh, no, it's time to go!

Chorus

**Go, go, go! Hurry, Kate!
Hurry, Kate! You can't be late!**

Kate eats breakfast, she gets dressed.
It's 7:45.
It's time to go to school.
And she can't be late!

Chorus

4 Read, match, and say. Ask and answer.

1 7:00   a seven forty-five
2 7:30   b seven fifty-five
3 7:45   c seven o'clock
4 7:55   d seven thirty
5 5:25   e five twenty-five
6 4:10   f four fifteen
7 4:15   g four ten

When does she wake up?

She wakes up at seven o'clock.

Which activities do you do inside?
Which do you do outside?

Unit 1   5

Story

I will read a story about daily routines and times.

5 Listen and read. What does Luke do after school?

I Love Mondays!

1. Luke wakes up and goes into the kitchen.

- Good morning, Mom! What day is it today?
- It's Monday.
- Hooray! I love Mondays!

2. Before school, Luke always eats breakfast.

- Before lunch, at eleven ten, I have art. Art is fun!
- But...

3. After breakfast, he brushes his teeth. Then he washes his face.

- We draw pictures. We paint. It's great!
- But today...

4. He gets dressed.

- After lunch, at two fifteen, we have English. I love English!
- But Luke...

6 **Read and say before school or after school.**

1 Luke eats breakfast.
2 Luke gets dressed.
3 Luke plays soccer.
4 Luke puts on his shoes.
5 Luke wakes up.
6 Luke plays basketball.

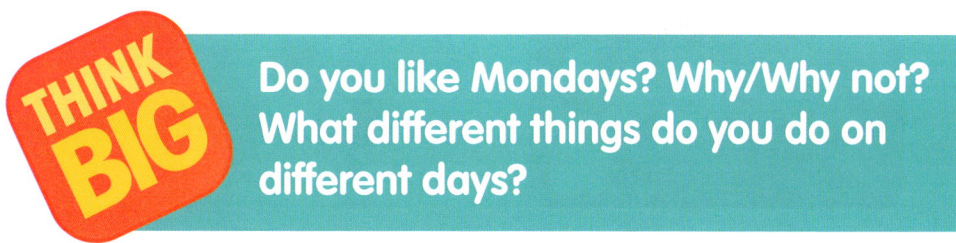

Do you like Mondays? Why/Why not? What different things do you do on different days?

Language in Action

I will listen to a dialog about daily routines and times.

7 🎧 **Listen and read. Then say.**

Jenna: Hi, Ethan. Do you want to get together after school today?

Ethan: Sorry, I can't. I'm busy on Tuesdays.

Jenna: Really? What do you do?

Ethan: At 3:30, I have piano lessons. At 4:15, I go to soccer practice. Then I go home.

Jenna: Oh. What do you do after that?

Ethan: I do my homework, clean my room, and feed the dog. Then at 7:00, we eat dinner.

Jenna: Wow! You *are* busy.

8 **Look at 5. Ask and answer with a partner.**

What does Luke do before school?

He wakes up, eats breakfast, …

9 🎧 **Listen and stick. Number the pictures.**

Grammar

I will learn to use *before* and *after* to ask and answer about daily routines.

What does he/she do **before/after** school?   He/She eats breakfast **before/after** school.

What do you do **before/after** school?   I do my homework **before/after** school.

10 Look at Claudia's schedule. Write **before** or **after**.

Claudia's Schedule

6:30	wake up	3:15	get home
6:45	get dressed	3:30	watch TV
7:00	eat breakfast	4:45	do my homework
7:15	brush my teeth	5:30	play soccer
7:30	go to school	6:30	eat dinner

1 Claudia gets dressed _____ school.
2 Claudia does her homework _____ school.
3 Claudia brushes her teeth _____ school.
4 Claudia plays soccer _____ school.
5 Claudia eats breakfast _____ school.

11 Read and match. Make sentences.

1 We eat breakfast before   a at 5:00 in the afternoon.
2 I wake up at   b we get dressed.
3 Paula washes her   c after school, at 4:15.
4 Tim does his homework   d face at 7:50 in the morning.
5 Sandra plays video games   e 6:45 in the morning.

12 Look at **10**. Talk about Claudia's schedule with a partner.

Claudia wakes up at 6:30 in the morning.

She gets dressed at 6:45.

Unit 1 9

Content Connection | Life Science

I will learn about keeping clean.

 Listen and read. What are bacteria?

Keep It Clean!

CONTENT WORDS
bacteria   cough
decay   germs
healthy   sick   sneeze

Take a Shower

When your parents tell you to take a shower, they are giving you good advice. Wash your face, behind your ears, and under your arms. Be sure to wash your whole body well. Use warm water and soap to wash away bacteria. Bacteria are tiny living things that can make you sick.

Brush Your Teeth

To keep your teeth strong and healthy, be sure to brush them twice a day. Brush in the morning when you wake up. And brush at night before you go to sleep. Brushing your teeth cleans away bacteria that can cause tooth decay. It's important to brush your teeth for at least two minutes at a time.

Wash Your Hands

Every day, our hands pick up millions of germs that can make us sick. Be sure to wash your hands with soap and water for at least twenty seconds. Wash your hands before you eat, after you visit the bathroom, after you cough or sneeze, and any other time your hands get dirty.

Washing your hands, showering, and brushing your teeth are three easy things you can do every day to keep yourself clean and healthy.

14 Look at 13. Read and circle **T** for true or **F** for false.

1. Bacteria can make you sick. **T   F**
2. Wash your hands only once a day. **T   F**
3. Wash your hands after you take a shower. **T   F**
4. Brush your teeth for at least two minutes at a time. **T   F**
5. Brush your teeth five times a day. **T   F**

 What other things can you do to stay healthy? Where can we learn about staying healthy?

10   Unit 1

Culture Connection | Around the World

I will learn about **time zones**.

15 Read and complete. Then listen and check.

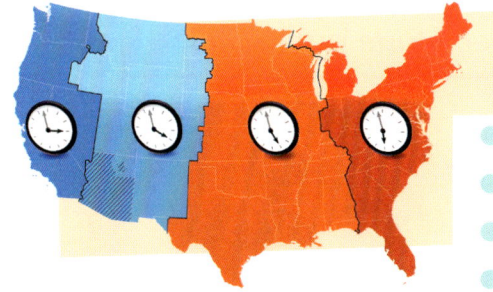

Time Zones

Do You Know What Time It Is?

Is it the same time everywhere in the world? No, it's not. That's because the world is divided into time zones. Look at the map of the United States. It has four different time zones.

1:00 in the afternoon

It's 1:00 in New York, and Manuel and his friends are finishing their lunch.

In Texas, it's 12:00, and Maria is just finishing math class.

John, in Montana, is hungry and is thinking about lunch. He looks at the clock. It's only 11:00 in the morning!

And for Kara, in California, it's only 10:00 in the morning.

two hours later

Now it's ____:00 in New York, and school is over. Manuel is playing soccer.

In Texas, it's ____:00, and Maria is still in school.

It's ____:00 in Montana, and John is finishing his lunch.

Kara, in California, looks at the clock, and it's ____:00. Hooray! It's lunchtime!

five more hours later

It is ____:00 at night now in New York, and Manuel is finishing his homework.

In Texas, it's ____:00, and Maria is eating dinner.

In Montana, it's now ____:00, and John is making dinner with his dad.

In California, Kara is playing with her sister. It's ____:00.

 New York
 Texas
 Montana
 California

16 Work with a partner. Ask and answer.

1 When it's 6:00 in the evening in Montana, what time is it in California?

2 Manuel wakes up at 7:00 in the morning. What is Kara doing when Manuel wakes up?

3 How many time zones does your country have?

 **THINK BIG** It's ten o'clock in the morning where you are. Find out what time it is in Buenos Aires, Cairo, and Sydney.

Unit 1

Writing | Sentence: Subjects and Verbs

I will learn to write sentences with subjects and verbs.

> A sentence has a **subject** and a **verb**.
>
> **She eats** breakfast before school.　　**I ride** my bike to school.
> *She* is the subject. *Eats* is the verb.　　*I* is the subject. *Ride* is the verb.

17 **Find the subjects and verbs. Compare with your partner.**

1 I watch TV at 5:15.
2 Marcia brushes her teeth at 7:45.
3 We play soccer in the afternoon.
4 They do their homework at 4:30.
5 You eat dinner with your family in the evening.

18 **What's missing, subject or verb? Complete the sentences and compare with a partner.**

> brother   cleans   She   Tom   wakes

1 Bridget _____ up at 6:45 in the morning.
2 _____ eats breakfast at 7:00.
3 Her _____ gets dressed at 7:15 in the morning.
4 Bridget _____ her room before school.
5 _____ plays video games after school.

19 **Write three sentences about your day. Read them to a partner.**

_____
_____
_____

12　Unit 1

Phonics | a_e, i_e, o_e

I will learn to use the sounds *a_e*, *i_e*, and *o_e*.

 Listen, read, and repeat.

1 **a_e**   2 **i_e**   3 **o_e**

 Listen and find. Then say.

  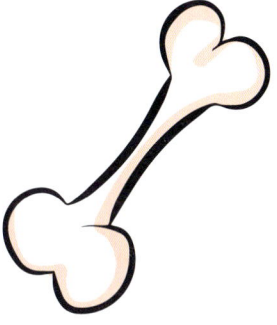

f**ace**   b**ike**   b**one**

 Listen and blend the sounds.

1 g-a-me   game   2 c-a-ke   cake
3 t-i-me   time   4 n-o-te   note
5 h-o-me   home   6 sh-a-pe   shape
7 r-i-de   ride   8 l-i-ke   like

 Read aloud. Then listen and chant.

What time is it?
It's time to play a game.
What time is it?
It's time to eat cake.
What time is it?
It's time to ride a bike.
What time is it?
It's time to go home.

Unit 1 13

Values | Do your chores.

I will learn to talk about chores.

 24 Look, listen, and point.

a
I feed the dog before school.

b
I clean my room after school.

c
I wash the dishes after dinner.

 Look at **24**. What might happen if they don't do their chores?

 Project

26 What chores do you do at home? Copy the chart in your notebook and ✓. Then ask three classmates about their chores.

CHORES

Chore	Me	1	2	3
feed pet				
clean my room				
wash the dishes				

Review

27 Read and circle.

Mia likes Fridays! She ¹**wakes / wake** up on Fridays at seven fifteen. She washes her ²**face / TV**, gets dressed, eats breakfast, and brushes her teeth ³**before / after** school. Mia likes school on Fridays. ⁴**Before / After** lunch, at 10:30, she has art class. She likes to draw! At 4:45 she ⁵**play / plays** video games with her friends – they always play ⁶**before / after** school. At 7:00 she ⁷**eat / eats** pizza with her family. She loves pizza!

28 Play the Silly Sentences game.

6:15 in the evening

eat breakfast

Jack eats breakfast at six fifteen in the evening.

That's silly!

I Can

- use words for daily activities.
- use *before* and *after* to talk about when things happen.
- talk about what I do every day.
- write sentences with subjects and verbs.

Unit 1

2 A Lot of Jobs!

Vocabulary

I will learn to name jobs.

🎵♪ Song Time! ♪🎵

1 Listen, look, and say.
Different Jobs

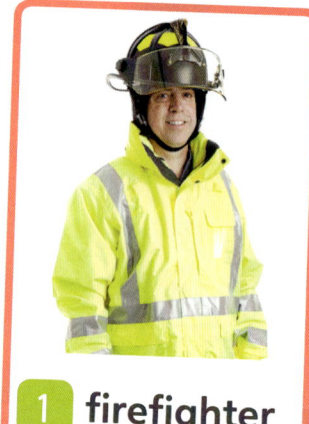
1 firefighter

2 chef

3 police officer

4 cashier

5 farmer

6 nurse

7 waiter

8 scientist

9 teacher

10 mail carrier

2 Play the speed game.

Song

I will learn to ask and answer about jobs and workplaces.

3 **Listen and sing. How many jobs are in the song?**

Working Together

There are many people
In our community.
So many jobs to do,
So many places to be.

**Working together, working hard.
Nurse, farmer, teacher, and chef.**

Where does she work?
What does she do?
She's a nurse,
And she always helps you.

Chorus
Where does he work?
What does he do?
He's a firefighter,
And he's very brave, too.

4 Match the jobs in 1 with the places. Make sentences.

a
at a hospital

b
at a store

c
at a fire station

d
at a school

e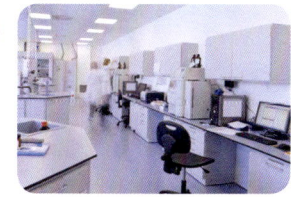
at a laboratory

f
at a police station

g
at a restaurant

h
on a farm

THINK BIG Which job is the most important?

> A teacher works at a school.

> A scientist works at a laboratory.

Unit 2 17

Story

I will read a story about jobs.

🎧 5 Listen and read. What does Luke's mom do?

Is She a Doctor?

1. Luke and his dad are at the hospital.

2. They want to find Luke's mom.

3. Luke's mom is at work.

4. Luke's mom works at the hospital.

6 **Read and complete the sentences. Then say.**

1 Luke is looking for his _____.
2 Luke's mom works at the _____.
3 Luke's mom isn't a doctor or a _____.
4 Luke's mom is a _____.
5 Today it's Luke's mom's _____.

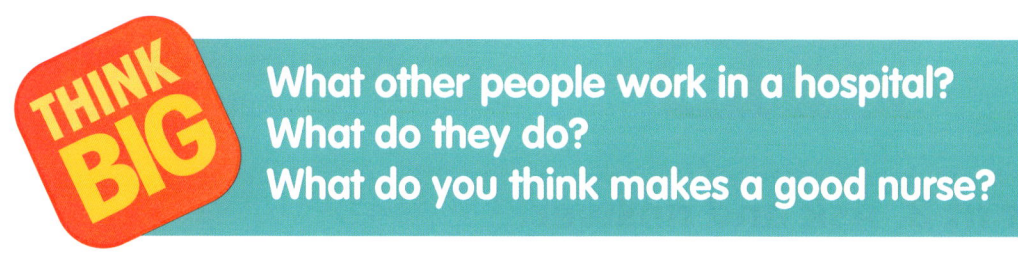

What other people work in a hospital?
What do they do?
What do you think makes a good nurse?

Language in Action

I will listen to a dialog about jobs.

7 **Listen and read. Then say.**

Emma: Where does your mom work?
Will: She works at a television station.
Emma: What does she do?
Will: She's a reporter.
Emma: That's really cool. I want to be a newspaper reporter someday. I love to write.
Will: You do? I don't. I want to be an artist. I love to draw!

8 **Listen and stick. Number the pictures.**

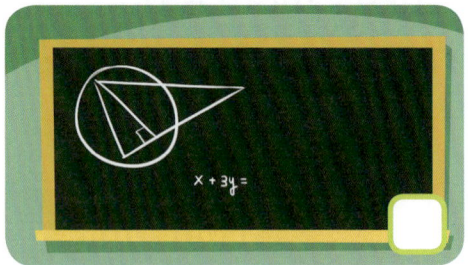

9 **Look at 8. Ask and answer.**

What does he do?

He's a barber.

20 Unit 2

Grammar

I will learn to use *what* and *where* to ask and answer about what people do and where they work.

What does he/she **do**?	He/She**'s** (He/She **is**) a firefighter.
Where does he/she **work**?	He/She **works** at a fire station.
What do your sisters **do**?	They**'re** (They **are**) chefs.

10 Complete the dialogs.

1. **A:** What does your dad _____?
   B: He's a chef.
   A: Where _____ he work?
   B: He _____ at a restaurant.

2. **A:** What _____ your sisters Melanie and Patricia do?
   B: _____ firefighters.
   A: Where do they work?
   B: They _____ at a fire station.

11 Number in order. Make a dialog.

A: What does your mom do? ☐
B: She works at a school. ☐
A: Where does she work? ☐
B: She's a nurse. ☐

12 Ask and answer questions like the ones in 10.

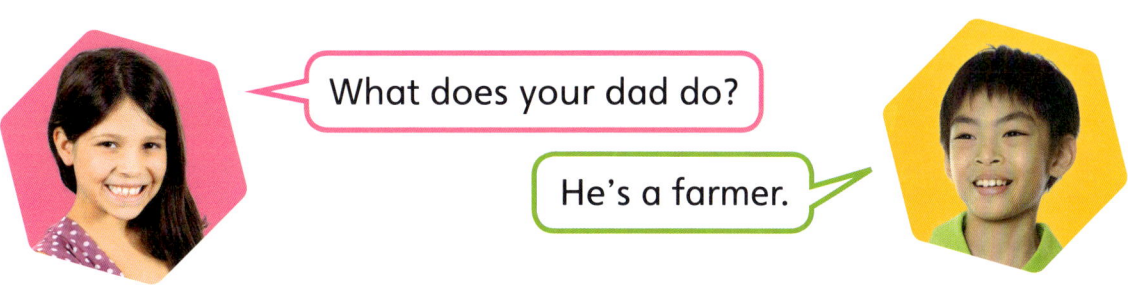

What does your dad do?

He's a farmer.

Unit 2 21

Content Connection | Social Science

I will learn about creative jobs.

CONTENT WORDS
create   drawings
galleries   materials
paintings   photo shoot
professional   work of art

13 Listen and read. Which of these people sell their work to magazines?

THE WORK FILES: Creative Jobs

People spend a big part of their lives at work, so it's very important to choose the right job. When you do something you really enjoy, you feel happy. Today we're taking a look at creative jobs. Would you like to do one of them?

Artist

Professional artists usually go to art school. They learn to use different materials to create a work of art. They use pencils to make drawings, oil paints, acrylics, or water colors to make paintings, and metal or wood to make other works of art. Artists show their work in art galleries. A work of art can be very expensive.

Photographer

Photographers travel a lot and take pictures of people and places all over the world. Their work is sometimes difficult or dangerous, like when they take pictures of wild animals. They sell their pictures to websites, newspapers, magazines, and television news shows. They also sell books with their pictures.

Fashion Designer

Fashion designers create the clothes we wear. First, they draw sketches with their ideas. Then they cut patterns to make dresses and many more things. Designing clothes can be a lot of fun. Fashion designers show their work in fashion shows or do photo shoots for magazines.

14 Interview a partner. Take notes in your notebook. Share with the class.

1 Do you like art? Do you have a favorite work of art?
2 What kinds of pictures do you like to look at (people, fashion, etc.)?
3 Do you like fashion? What kinds of clothes do you usually wear?

What other creative jobs can you think of? What talents do you need to do a creative job?

Culture Connection | Around the World

I will learn about community volunteering.

CONTENT WORDS
be proud of   collect   community   contest   donate   get lost   trash

15 Listen and read. Who helps tourists in their city?

Making Communities Better

Here are three stories of kids working hard to make their communities better.

Lalana lives in Chiang Mai, Thailand. She knows that many schools in her city don't have money to buy books. Lalana and her friends ask people to donate books. They collect the books and take them to schools in their city.

Lalana

Marcus

Marcus lives in a small town near Melbourne, Australia. Every morning he walks to school. He sees a lot of trash along the road. He and his friends have a contest. They pick up the trash, and they see who can collect the most.

Carla lives in Barcelona, Spain. A lot of tourists visit her city every year, and they often get lost. Carla likes helping people, and she's proud of her city. On the weekends, she and her big sister help tourists find the places they're looking for.

Carla

16 Look at **15**. Correct the mistakes. Make new sentences.

1. In Chiang Mai, schools donate books to people.
2. Barcelona doesn't have many tourists.
3. Marcus rides his bike to school.

THINK BIG — Talk to your friends. How can you help your community?

Writing | Sentence: Compound Subjects and Verbs

I will learn to write sentences with two subjects or two verbs.

> A sentence can have a compound subject.
> Al is a farmer. Pat is a farmer. → **Al and Pat are** farmers.
>
> A sentence can have a compound verb.
> I live in Rome. I work in Rome. → I **live and work** in Rome.

17 Use and to make sentences with compound subjects or compound verbs.

1 Lily is a scientist. Tom is a scientist.
   _____

2 My mother is a teacher. My father is a teacher.
   _____

3 I work at the restaurant. I eat at the restaurant.
   _____

4 My sister lives on a farm. My brother lives on a farm.
   _____

5 My grandfather lives in an apartment building. My grandfather works in an apartment building.
   _____

18 Complete the sentences for you. Then say.

1 Before school, I _____ and _____.
2 After school, I _____ and _____.

Before school, I eat breakfast and get dressed.

After school, I play soccer and do my homework.

Phonics | sm, st, sp, sk

I will learn to use the sounds *sm*, *st*, *sp*, and *sk*.

 **19 Listen, read, and repeat.**

1 **sm**   2 **st**   3 **sp**   4 **sk**

 20 Listen and find. Then say.

smile   **st**op   **sp**oon   **sk**ates

 **21 Listen and blend the sounds.**

1 s-m-ar-t	smart	2 s-k-i-n	skin
3 S-p-ai-n	Spain	4 s-m-o-ke	smoke
5 s-k-i	ski	6 s-t-or-m	storm
7 s-t-ar	star	8 s-p-a-ce	space

22 Read aloud. Then listen and chant.

Stop and look.
Look at the stars,
The stars in space,
And smile!

Unit 2 25

Values | Respect others.

I will learn to talk about respecting others.

23 **Look, listen, and point.**

24 Look at **23**. Role-play with a partner.

25 Make a class book about respecting others.

Listen to your teacher.

Respect police officers.

Review

26 **Complete the sentences. Use the words from the box.**

| cashier   farm   laboratory   nurse   police station   teacher |

1 I'm a farmer. I work on a _____.
2 My brother is a _____. He works at a school.
3 My dad is a police officer. He works at a _____.
4 My grandmother is a _____. She works at a store.
5 My grandfather is a scientist. He works in a _____.
6 My uncle is a _____. He works at a hospital.

27 **Play the Jobs game.**

I Can

- use job words.
- use *what* and *where* to ask and answer about what people do and where they work.
- talk about what people do and where they work.
- write sentences with compound subjects or verbs.

Unit 2   27

3 Working Hard!

Vocabulary

I will learn to name chores.

1 Listen, look, and say.

1 make my bed

2 walk the dog

3 practice the piano

4 take out the trash

5 do the dishes

6 clean my room

7 study for a test

8 feed the fish

2 Play the acting game.

28 Unit 3

Song

I will learn to ask and answer about chores.

3 **Listen and sing. What chores does Matt do?**

Different Twins

My name's Matt,
And my name's Mike.
We want to talk to you.
I do my chores,
And I do, too.
But we are not alike.

**Mike and Matt, Matt and Mike.
These two twins are not alike.**

I'm Matt, I always clean my room.
I do my chores each day.
I sometimes do the dishes,
And then we go and play.

Chorus
I'm Mike, I always make my bed.
I do my chores each day.
I sometimes walk the dog,
And then we go and play.

Chorus

4 **Use the chart to ask and answer questions about Matt.**

Matt	Sun	Mon	Tue	Wed	Thu	Fri	Sat
clean his room	✓	✓	✓	✓	✓	✓	✓
feed the fish	✓	✓		✓		✓	✓
do the dishes	✓				✓		
take out the trash							

Does Matt clean his room?

Yes, he does.

**Which of these are your favorite chores?
Why are chores important?**

Story

I will read a story about chores.

5. Listen and read. What time does Amy have to leave for school?

I Have a Lot to Do

1. Amy is thinking. Her mom comes into her bedroom.
   - Hey, Amy...!
   - Yes? I'm busy!

2. Amy likes making lists. She often makes a list of things she has to do.
   - You're always busy! What are you doing?
   - I have to do a lot of things today. I'm making a list.

3. Amy has to do a lot of things before school.
   - What do you have to do?
   - I have to eat breakfast and brush my teeth. Then I have to feed the fish, clean my room, and study for my math test.

4. Amy's clock still says 7:05.
   - What time do you have to leave for school?
   - I always leave at 7:50. Why?

5 You have to get a new alarm clock, too. It's 7:45!
What time does Amy have to leave? At 7:50? Oh, no!

6 What? Oh, no! I have to go!
Good luck!
Amy's never late for school. She doesn't want to be late today!

6 Read and say true or false.

1 Amy has to do a lot of things before school.
2 She has to eat breakfast.
3 She has to walk the dog.
4 She has to study for her English test.
5 She has to leave for school at 7:00.
6 She has to get a new alarm clock.

Do you make lists?
What kinds of lists do people make?
How do lists help us remember things?
What other things help us remember?

Language in Action

I will listen to a dialog about chores.

7 **Listen and read. Then say.**

Amy: Hey, Betsy, do you want to go skating after school today?

Betsy: Sorry, but I can't today. I have to go to my piano lesson.

Amy: Piano lesson?

Betsy: Uh-huh. I always have a piano lesson on Tuesday afternoons.

Amy: Oh, OK. How about tomorrow?

Betsy: Sure. Sounds great!

8 Look at **7**. Role-play with a partner.

9 **Listen and stick.**

Monday	Tuesday	Wednesday	Thursday	Friday

10 What about you? Ask and answer.

What do you have to do?

I have to practice the piano on Mondays.

Grammar

I will learn to use *have to* to talk about chores.
I will learn to use *always*, *usually*, *sometimes*, and *never* to talk about chores.

| What **does** he/she **have to** do? | He/She **has to** feed the fish. |
| What **do** you/we/they **have to** do? | I/We/They **have to** eat breakfast. |

11 Complete the dialogs.

1 **A:** What _____ you have to do in the morning?
   B: I _____ make my bed every morning.

2 **A:** What _____ Ted have to do after school?
   B: Ted _____ practice the piano.

| I/You/We/They | always
usually | do the dishes. |
| He/She | sometimes
never | takes out the trash. |

12 Look at the chart. Write sentences about Leo.

Leo's chores	Mon	Tue	Wed	Thu	Fri
make his bed	✓		✓		
do his homework	✓	✓	✓	✓	✓
clean his room					

1 _____
2 _____
3 _____

13 Work with a partner. Ask and answer.

Do you always do the dishes?

Yes, I always do the dishes.

Unit 3   33

Content Connection | Math

I will learn about pocket money.

CONTENT WORDS
adult   cash   cost   earn   let (someone) know   save   stranger

14 **Listen and read. Who can you work for?**

Pocket Money

When you want to buy something expensive, you need extra money. Where do you find it? You can't get a real job yet, but there are ways you can earn some extra cash.

Help with the housework Everyone has to help around the house. You probably have to clean your room and take out the trash. Do extra work to earn extra money. Ask your parents what extra things you can do for them and how much they can pay you for doing them.

Do chores for other people Sometimes other adult members of your family, friends, or neighbors are very busy, and they don't have time to do some chores. Let them know how you can help. Write what you can do and how much it costs on a piece of paper, make copies, and give them to the people you know. Remember to be safe. Don't work for strangers. Always ask your parents and let them know where you are.

Save your money Save a little bit of the money you make every time. This way you always have extra cash!

15 **Ask and answer.**

Do you help with the housework to earn extra money?

I do! Do you do chores for other people?

THINK BIG Is it better to spend or save pocket money? Why? How much of your pocket money should you save?

34   Unit 3

Culture Connection | Around the World

I will learn about chores of the past.

CONTENT WORDS
bucket   fire   forest   handle   lamp   oil   pump   stove   wind   wood

16 Listen and read. What chores do these children do?

Chores from Long Ago

Joseph Macgill, United States: I have to carry wood into the house. We use the wood to make a fire. The fire keeps us warm, and we also use it to cook our food. Every summer my dad and I go to the forest and cut trees. Then we chop the trees into smaller pieces of wood. It's hard to carry wood—it's heavy!

Sarah Donaldson, Australia: I have to get water for my family. We have a pump outside. I move the pump handle up and down. After a minute, water comes out. The water goes into a bucket, and I carry the bucket inside. We all use the water for drinking, cooking, and bathing. When we want hot water, we put some in a pot, and heat it on the stove.

Annabelle Dubois, France: Every night before I go to bed, I have to wind our clock. You have to use a special key to wind the clock. If you don't wind the clock every day, it stops working. It's not a very interesting chore, but it's a very important one! Then I fill lamps with oil. We need oil in the lamps to make light. We use the lamps at night to read books and do our homework.

17 Ask your classmates what chores they have to do to help their family. Make a list.

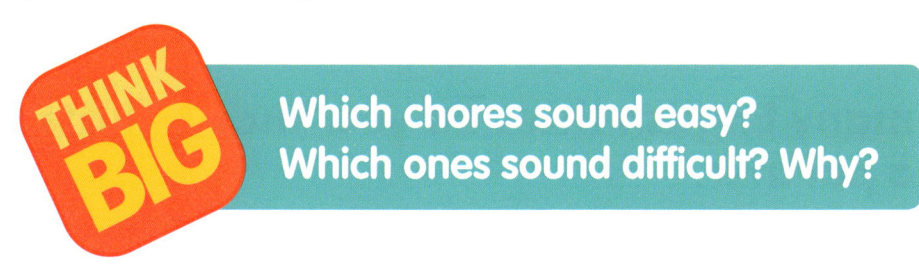

THINK BIG: Which chores sound easy? Which ones sound difficult? Why?

Unit 3   35

Writing | Paragraph: Titles

I will learn to write paragraph titles.

Use capital letters for most words in titles.
Taking Care of a Big Dog

18 **Find the words we don't capitalize in the titles.**

Good Things to Eat

My Brother and I

The Big Blue Car

A Day at the Park with Grandma

To the Moon and Back

19 **Rewrite the titles. Use capital letters as needed.**

1 my sister's new job
_____

2 lots of chores for my brother
_____

3 helping out around the house
_____

4 a strange day out
_____

5 the jobs kids like the best
_____

6 helping my family is fun
_____

7 helping my dad
_____

20 **How many English titles do you know? Write them with a partner.**

36 Unit 3

Phonics | ay, oy

I will learn to use the sounds *ay* and *oy*.

21 Listen, read, and repeat.
1 ay   2 oy

22 Listen and find. Then say.

May   toy

23 Listen and blend the sounds.
1 d-ay   day   2 j-oy   joy
3 s-ay   say   4 p-ay   pay
5 b-oy   boy   6 s-oy   soy
7 w-ay   way   8 r-ay   ray

24 Read aloud. Then listen and chant.

What do we say?
It's May, it's May,
It's a nice day.
Come on, girls!
Come on, boys!
Bring your toys.

Unit 3 37

Values | Always be happy to help.

I will learn to talk about helping others.

25 **Look and listen. Are they happy to help? Say yes or no.**

1. Can you help me? — Sure!

2. Hey, I need some help! — Now? I'm watching TV.

3. Come help me, please. — OK. I'm coming, Grandma!

26 Role-play the dialogs in **25** with a partner.

Project

27 Make a sock puppet. With a partner, use your puppet to role-play helping someone.

Can you help me study for my spelling test? — Sure!

38 Unit 3

Review

28 Complete the sentences. Use the words from the box.

> do   have to   has to   have   study

1 What _____ they _____ to do?
2 Larry _____ help his parents after school.
3 Paolo has to _____ for a test.
4 Sammy and Todd _____ do the dishes.

29 Fill in the chart. Ask a partner about his/her chores. Use **always**, **usually**, **sometimes**, or **never**.

My chores	Sun	Mon	Tue	Wed	Thu	Fri	Sat
1 I _____ clean my room.							
2 I _____ do my homework.							
3 I _____ do the dishes.							
4 I _____ help my parents.							

Do you always do the dishes?

No, I sometimes do the dishes.

I Can

- use words for chores and other kinds of work.
- use *have to* to talk about how often people do things.
- use *always, usually, sometimes,* and *never* to talk about chores.
- use capital letters in titles.

Unit 3 **39**

Checkpoint | Units 1–3

How well do I know it? Can I use it?

1 **Think about it. Read and circle. Practice.**

I know this.   I don't know this.

I need more practice.

1. **Daily activities:** eat breakfast, watch TV, practice the piano... — p. 4, 28

2. **Telling time:** one o'clock, two thirty, 5:15... — p. 5

3. **Jobs:** waiter, firefighter, nurse... — p. 16

4. **Workplaces:** police station, restaurant, laboratory... — p. 17

5. What does he do **before** school?
He washes his face **before** school.
What do you do **after** school?
I play video games **after** school. — p. 9

6. **What does** he do?
He **is** a cashier.
Where does he work?
He **works** at a store. — p. 21

7. What **do** they **have to** do?
They **have to** feed the fish. — p. 33

8. They **always/usually/sometimes/never** do their homework after school. — p. 33

I can do it!

🎧 Get ready.

A. Complete the interview. Use the words from the box. Then listen and check.

> Do you eat dinner at home?
> usually
> What do you do?
> What do you do before work?
> When do you go to work?
> Where do you work?

Katy: ¹_____

Max: I'm a chef.

Katy: Oh, really? ²_____

Max: I work at a restaurant, the Pizza Palace.

Katy: I see. ³_____

Max: I ⁴_____ go to work at 2:00. I come home at 11:00 at night.

Katy: OK. ⁵_____

Max: I take a shower, eat breakfast, and get dressed. Then I feed my fish.

Katy: ⁶_____

Max: No, I always eat dinner at the restaurant.

B. Make more questions.

1 When _____ ?
2 _____ before work?
3 _____ in the afternoon?

C. Practice the dialog in **A** with a partner. Include your new questions.

Checkpoint Units 1–3   **41**

Checkpoint | Units 1–3

3 **Get set.**

STEP 1 Choose a job.

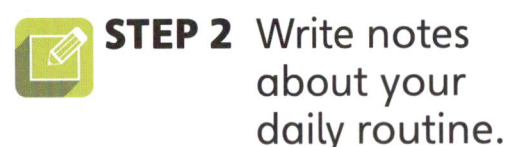

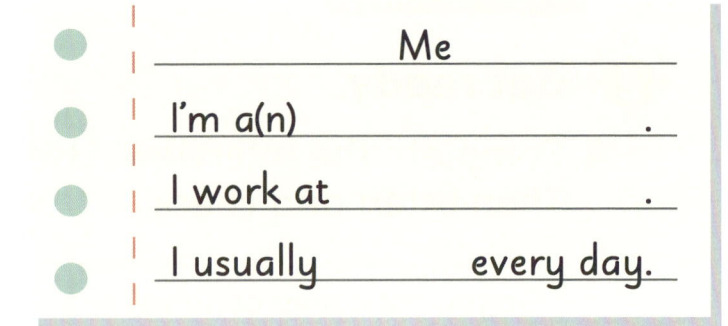

STEP 2 Write notes about your daily routine.

_____ Me
I'm a(n) _____ .
I work at _____ .
I usually _____ every day.

STEP 3 Cut out the cards on page **133**. Now you're ready to **Go**!

4 **Go!**

A. Use the cards to make questions. Interview your partner. Write about your partner's daily routine. Then switch roles.

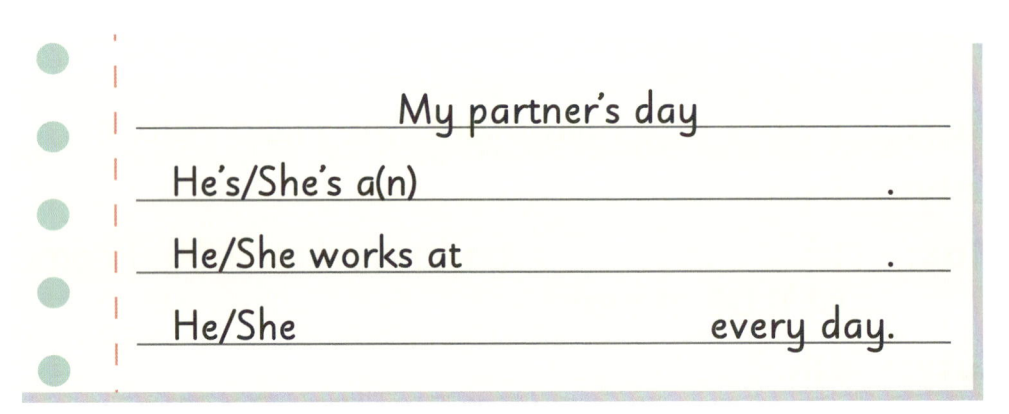

_____ My partner's day _____
He's/She's a(n) _____ .
He/She works at _____ .
He/She _____ every day.

B. Work in groups. Tell your classmates about your partner's daily routine.

> Luisa always eats breakfast before school.

5 **Write about yourself in your notebook.**
- When do you wake up?
- What do you do before school?
- What chores do you have to do?
- What time do you go to bed?

All About Me

_____
_____
_____

How well do I know it now?

6 **Think about it.**

A. Go to page 40. Look and circle again.

B. Check (✔).
- ☐ I can start the next unit.
- ☐ I can ask my teacher for help and then start the next unit.
- ☐ I can practice and then start the next unit.

7 **Rate this Checkpoint. Color.**

hard   OK   easy | not fun   OK   fun

Checkpoint Units 1–3

4 Amazing Animals

Vocabulary

I will learn to name animals.

🎵 **Song Time!** 🎵

1 Listen, look, and say.

1 bear	2 deer	3 owl
4 camel	5 lizard	6 penguin
7 toucan	8 sea lion	9 shark

2 Play the description game.

44 Unit 4

Song

I will learn to ask and answer about animals and where they live.

3 Listen and sing. How many animals are in the song?

Animals Are Amazing!

Animals are amazing!
We see them far and near.
Some live in forests
Like owls, bears, and deer.
Some live in deserts
Like camels and some snakes.
Some live in water,
In oceans, seas, and lakes.

Amazing, amazing animals
What can animals do?
They can fly, they can swim, they can jump!
We share the earth with you!

4 Match the animals with the places. Ask and answer.

> deserts   forests   ice and snow   jungles
> lakes   mountains   oceans   rain forests

Where do lizards live?

Some live in deserts and some live in lakes.

THINK BIG Look at the pictures. Which is your favorite animal and why?

Unit 4 45

Story

I will read a story about animals.

5. Listen and read. Can Smartie talk?

At the Zoo

1 Luke and Amy are watching a sea lion show at the zoo.

- Amy, look at that sea lion. It's clapping to the music!
- Oh, cool!

2 Luke has to cover his ears.

- Now it's trying to sing. What an awful sound!
- Sea lions can't sing very well.

3 The sea lion can balance a ball on its nose!

- Now it's balancing a ball!
- Sea lions can do some great tricks!

4 Then Luke and Amy watch a parrot show.

- What can parrots do?
- Wow, parrots can ride bikes!

46 Unit 4

5 The parrot's name is Smartie.

6 When Smartie starts talking, Smartie can't stop!

Speech bubbles:
- Hello, Smartie. Good bird! Can you talk?
- Hello, Smartie. Good bird! Can you talk?
- Wow! Parrots can talk!
- Hello, Smartie. Good bird. Can you talk? Smartie can talk.
- Smartie can't stop talking!

6 Read and match. Make sentences.

1 Sea lions can't   a stop talking.
2 Sea lions can   b parrot.
3 Smartie is a   c say its name.
4 Smartie can   d sing very well.
5 Smartie can't   e do great tricks.

THINK BIG
What other animals are very smart?
What can they do?
What different ways are there to learn about animals in a zoo?

Unit 4   47

Language in Action

I will listen to a dialog about animals.

7. Listen and read. Then say.

Brad: Are you ready for an animal quiz?
Samuel: Yes, I am!
Brad: OK. Listen. This animal lives in the ice and snow. It can swim, but it can't fly.
Samuel: I know! It's a penguin.
Brad: Right! Now it's your turn.
Samuel: OK. Let's see… It lives in the forest. It can climb trees, and it can swim.
Brad: Hmm… Is it a snake?
Samuel: No. It has four legs, and it can run fast.
Brad: Oh, I know. It's a bear!
Samuel: That's right!

8. Listen and stick. Number the pictures.

9. Make statements. Then say true or false.

Sharks can run and swim.

False! Sharks can't run but they can swim.

48 Unit 4

Grammar

I will learn to use *can* to ask and answer about animals.

What **can** a bear do?	It **can** swim. It **can't** fly.	subject + *can/can't* + verb
What **can** owls do?	They **can** fly. They **can't** climb.	
Can a penguin jump?	Yes, it **can**./No, it **can't**.	subject + *can/can't*
Can lizards swim?	Yes, they **can**./No, they **can't**.	

10 Complete the sentences. Use can or can't.

1 Ducks and sea lions _____ swim.
2 A shark _____ climb a tree.
3 A giraffe _____ reach the leaves at the top of a tree.
4 A penguin _____ fly, but a toucan _____.
5 A parrot _____ talk, but a lizard _____.

11 Look at 1. Write questions and answers. Add one of your own!

1 Where do bears live?
   _____
2 Where do penguins live?
   _____
3 _____
   They live in the ocean.
4 _____
   They live in the rain forest.
5 _____
   _____

Unit 4

Content Connection | Life Science

I will learn about animal camouflage.

CONTENT WORDS
blend in   bottom of the ocean   hide   hunt   stone   tree bark

🎧 12 **Listen, read, and match the pictures with the paragraphs.**

Many animals blend in with their surroundings. This is called camouflage. Camouflage helps animals in different ways. Some use it to find food, but others use it because they don't want to become food!

Animal Camouflage

a b c

1 Polar Bears Hide in the Snow
Polar bears, for example, are found in the ice and snow. Everything around them is white. They're covered in white fur, but their eyes, noses, and the bottoms of their feet are black. When they hunt for food, they sometimes cover their eyes and nose with their paws.

2 Not a Stone, But a Stonefish
Stonefish use camouflage to get food. They look like stones on the bottom of the ocean. If a fish touches a stonefish by mistake, it stings them to death and eats them.

3 Tree Frogs Can't Be Seen
Gray tree frogs, however, use camouflage to hide. They're found in the forests of North America. Because they live in trees, they look like a tree branch.

13 Which animal uses camouflage to hide? Which animals use camouflage to hunt?

THINK BIG
Do you know any other animals that use camouflage? Where do they live? What do they look like? How do they blend in?

50   Unit 4

Culture Connection | Around the World

I will learn about pets around the world.

14 Listen and read. Then complete the chart.

Pets in Different Places

Many people around the world have pets. Every country has its favorites. In the United States, there are about 93 million pet cats. Cats are very popular in China, too. Birds and goldfish are also popular. Birds such as the colorful parakeet are popular in Mexico. Parakeets like playing with people, and they can talk! In Italy, lots of people have canaries. Canaries can sing all day!

One of Japan's popular pets is the bunny rabbit. There are even bunny cafés where you can have coffee and spend time with these furry animals or buy one!

Some people choose unusual or exotic pets. Chilean Rose Hair Tarantulas are quiet and easy to keep, but they aren't very cuddly. There are millions of reptile pet owners around the world. Reptiles such as iguanas or geckos aren't dangerous, but snakes or alligators can be very dangerous, so pet owners need to be extra careful.

CONTENT WORDS
alligators   canaries   geckos
goldfish   parakeets
snakes   tarantulas

Popular pets	Unusual pets	Dangerous pets
_____	_____	_____

15 What are the popular pets in your country? Talk with a partner.

THINK BIG Is it a good idea to have wild animals as pets?

Unit 4 51

Writing | Paragraph: Topic Sentences

I will learn to write topic sentences.

> A **topic sentence** tells the main idea of a paragraph.
> My favorite pet is my snake, Cornwall.

16 Listen and read. What's Cornwall like?

title → **My Favorite Pet**
by Aaron Michaels

topic sentence → My favorite pet is my snake, Cornwall. He is a corn snake. He is 50 centimeters long, and he is red and white. I feed him one small mouse every week. He is friendly. He does not bite people. Some people don't like snakes, but snakes can make good pets.

17 Read and match the titles with the topic sentences.

Title
1 A Day at the Zoo
2 My Mother's Job
3 My Favorite Class
4 After-School Jobs
5 Our Pets

Topic Sentence
a My sister and I have many pets at home.
b My favorite time of day at school is art class.
c I have many jobs to do at home after school.
d My mother is a chef at an Italian restaurant.
e When I go to the zoo, I spend the whole day there.

18 What is your favorite animal? Write a title and a topic sentence.

_____

_____

Phonics | ea, oi, oe

I will learn to use the sounds *ea*, *oi*, and *oe*.

19 **Listen, read, and repeat.**

1 ea   2 oi   3 oe

20 **Listen and find. Then say.**

eat    coin 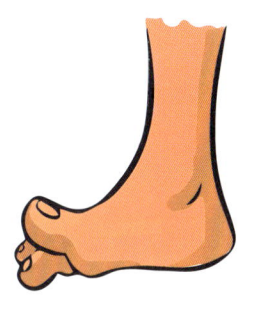   toe

21 **Listen and blend the sounds.**

1 s-ea   sea   2 b-oi-l   boil
3 b-ea-n bean   4 t-ea   tea
5 p-ea-ch peach   6 m-ea-t   meat
7 oi-l   oil   8 f-oe   foe

22 **Read aloud. Then listen and chant.**

So, Joe, boil the beans,
Add the oil,
Add the meat.
Eat the beans,
Eat the meat,
Eat the peach,
And drink the tea.

Unit 4 53

Values | Protect animals and their habitats.

I will learn to talk about protecting animals and their habitats.

23 Look at the map of animals in Australia. Play a game.

Animals of Australia

dingo (grasslands)
koala (forest)
kangaroo (desert)
parrot (rain forest)
kookaburra (forest)

Parrots in Australia live in the desert.

Wrong! They live in rain forests.

Project

24 Work in a group. Make an **Animals Map**.
- Choose a continent.
- Research the animals that live there.
- Draw and label your part of the map.

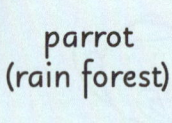

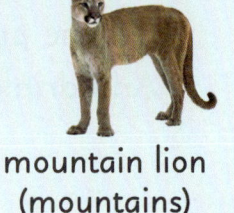

parrot (rain forest)
penguin (ice and snow)
snake (rain forest)
lizard (rain forest)
bear (forest)
mountain lion (mountains)

Review

25 Think about the animals you know. Complete the chart.

These animals can swim.	These animals can fly.
1	1
2	2
3	3
4	4

26 Complete the dialog. Then ask and answer.

Daniel: Where do sharks live?
Teresa: ¹ _____.
Daniel: Right. ² _____?
Teresa: Camels live in the desert.
Daniel: Right again! ³ _____?
Teresa: Camels can walk and run a little, but they can't jump or fly.
Daniel: How about penguins? Can they swim and fly?
Teresa: ⁴ _____.
Daniel: That's right!

27 Make sentences about sea lions and lizards.

What can they do?
What can't they do?
Where are they found?

I Can

- use words for animals and where they live.
- use *can* to ask and answer questions about what animals can do.
- talk about what animals can do and where they live.
- write topic sentences.

Unit 4   55

5 Wonderful Weather!

Vocabulary

I will learn to name types of weather.

🎵 **Song Time!** 🎵

1 Listen, look, and say.

The Weather today

1 It's windy.	**2** It's cold and snowy.

hot / warm / cool / cold

3 It's cool and cloudy.	**4** It's hot and sunny.	**5** It's warm and rainy.

2 Play the word game.

Unit 5

Song

I will learn to ask and answer about the weather and clothes.

3 Listen and sing. What's the weather like today?

Cool Weekend!

What's the weather like today?
Rainy, sunny, hot, or cold?

On Sunday, it was rainy,
It was very cold, too.
I was nice and warm in my winter coat,
Outside the sky wasn't blue!

Now it's Monday. It's sunny.
Great! I can go out and play.
Oh, no! I have to go to school.
Never mind! The weekend was cool!

Chorus (x2)

4 Listen and number. Then ask and answer for you.

- sunglasses
- shorts
- sandals
- sweater
- scarf
- raincoat
- umbrella
- boots
- hat
- coat
- gloves

What do you wear on sunny days?

On sunny days, I wear shorts, a T-shirt, and sunglasses.

THINK BIG

What do you do in good weather?
What weather is good for...
a soccer practice?
b a walk in the park?
c going to the beach?
d going skiing?

Unit 5 57

Story

I will read a story about the weather and clothes.

5. Listen and read. Where is Amy going today?

Amy is Ready!

1. I'm ready for my hike. I have my hiking boots, water, and snacks.

Amy is happy. Today her class is going on a hike.

2. Wait a minute! You need your raincoat and umbrella.

Why? What's the weather like? Is it rainy?

Mom doesn't think Amy is ready.

3. No, not right now. But what was the weather like yesterday?

It was rainy.

Mom doesn't want Amy to get wet.

4. And last night, it was cold and windy. Take your sweater. And your hat and gloves, too.

OK...

She doesn't want Amy to get cold.

58 Unit 5

> But, Mom, it's warm and sunny today!

> Sunny? Oh, then take your sunglasses and sunscreen, too!

> Now you're ready!

5 Amy isn't worried about the weather.

6 Amy is ready for all kinds of weather!

6 **Look at the story. Answer the questions with a partner.**

1 What's Amy's class doing today?
2 What was the weather like yesterday?
3 What was the weather like last night?
4 What's the weather like today?
5 What's Amy wearing at the end of the story?

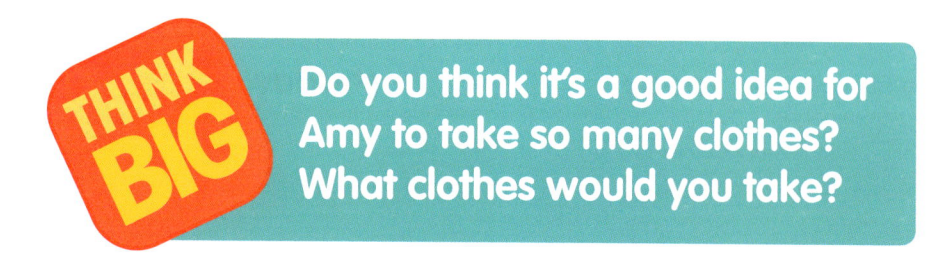

THINK BIG Do you think it's a good idea for Amy to take so many clothes? What clothes would you take?

Unit 5 59

Language in Action

I will listen to a dialog about the weather.

7. Listen and read. Then say.

Mom: Eli, you can't go out dressed like that!

Eli: But, Mom, it's not cold. It's just rainy.

Mom: It's windy, too. I don't want you to get sick. Please wear your raincoat.

Eli: Aww, Mom. I hate that raincoat.

Mom: What's wrong with that raincoat?

Eli: Everyone knows it was my sister's. I can't wear a girl's clothes.

Mom: Wear it today, and you can get a new raincoat.

Eli: A boy's raincoat?

Mom: Yes.

Eli: It's a deal.

8. Look at 7. Role-play with a partner.

9. Listen and stick.

San Francisco	
Yesterday	Today

Puerto Rico	
Yesterday	Today

60 Unit 5

Grammar

I will learn to to use *is* and *was* to ask and answer about the weather *today* and *yesterday*.

What **is** the weather like today?	It**'s** hot and sunny.
What **was** the weather like yesterday?	It **was** windy. Leaves **were** everywhere.

10 **Look at the calendar. Write sentences about the weather.**

M	T	W	Th	F
❄️	🌧️	☁️	🍂	☀️

1 Today is Friday. _____
2 Today is Monday. _____
3 Today is Tuesday. _____
4 Today is Wednesday. _____
5 Today is Thursday. _____

11 **Complete the dialog.**

A: Yesterday was great. We ¹_____ at the beach all day.

B: What ²_____ the weather like?

A: It ³_____ warm. What ⁴_____ the weather like today?

B: It ⁵_____ rainy and cool. We can't go to the beach today.

12 **How's the weather? Ask and answer questions with a partner.**

How's the weather today?

It's sunny and cool.

Unit 5 61

Content Connection | Geography

I will learn about different climates.

CONTENT WORDS
average   climate   degrees   Celsius   desert   dry   extreme   mild   minus

13 Listen and read. Which place is the coldest?

Changing Climates

The year-round weather in a place is called climate. It isn't the same for every place on the planet, and it usually changes with the seasons. In Southern Europe, for example, winters are usually mild. It often rains, but it doesn't snow much. Summers are generally dry and warm.

The Lut Desert in Iran is very hot and dry all year round. The temperatures there can be 70 degrees Celsius! Because of the extreme temperatures, some parts of the Lut desert have no life at all. Now you know why not many people go there!

It rains almost every day in Lloró, Colombia. Lloró gets an average of 13 meters of rain every year. That's a lot! The trees grow very quickly because of the wet climate.

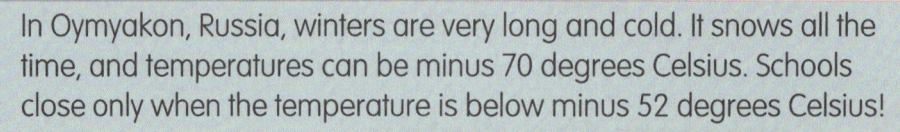

In Oymyakon, Russia, winters are very long and cold. It snows all the time, and temperatures can be minus 70 degrees Celsius. Schools close only when the temperature is below minus 52 degrees Celsius!

Places with a good climate are very popular. But a lot of sun and high temperatures isn't everyone's idea of a good climate. Some people really like the cold or wet weather. So long as everyone's happy!

14 Read and match.

1 Southern Europe   a extreme cold
2 Lut Desert, Iran   b lots of rain
3 Lloró, Colombia   c mild winters
4 Oymyakon, Russia   d very hot and dry

THINK BIG What difficulties do people who live in extreme climates have?

Culture Connection | Around the World

I will learn about weather around the world.

CONTENT WORDS

average   hot springs   rain forest   rink   sand dunes   temperature   tropical

15 Listen and read. What can you do on Mt. Seorak? Then match the titles with the paragraphs.

Summer? Winter? Both!

1 Do you like to go snowboarding? If you go to Huacachina, Peru, you can go snowboarding in the desert! In Huacachina, there are sand dunes almost 45 meters tall. You can ride to the top of the sand dunes in a jeep, and then hop on your snowboard and ride down the sand to the bottom of the hill. But be careful! If you fall, the sand can hurt – a lot! Make sure you wear a helmet and boots.

2 In Cornwall, in the United Kingdom, you can enjoy summer weather anytime. The Eden Project has a 50-meter tall biome with a rain forest inside. Visitors can see more than 1,000 types of plants and trees. In some parts of the biome, it can be 35°C! That probably feels good in the winter when it's only 6°C outside. The biome has four different types of rain forests: tropical islands, Southeast Asia, West Africa, and tropical South America.

3 Mt. Seorak is one of the most famous mountains in South Korea. People visit the mountain all year round, but winter is a special time here. You can go skiing on the mountain, but you can also go swimming at a water park. Seorak Waterpia has swimming pools filled with water from natural hot springs. The water has minerals in it, and many people say it is good for your health.

4 In the summer, the average temperature in Abu Dhabi, in the United Arab Emirates, is 42°C. Members of the Abu Dhabi Ice Sports Club can go ice skating all year. At the club, you can take ice skating lessons, watch figure skating shows, or even play ice hockey. The indoor ice skating rink feels great on a hot summer day.

a **Ice in the Desert**   b *Indoor Rain Forest*
c **Snowboarding on the Sand**   d **Swimming or Skiing?**

THINK BIG What activities do you do in the summer? What do you do in the winter?

Unit 5   63

Writing | Paragraph: Detail Sentences

I will learn to write detail sentences.

Here is a **topic sentence**.
  My favorite season is summer.
After the topic sentence, give more information. Write **detail sentences**.
  In the summer where I live, the weather is usually sunny and hot. I like to go to the beach with my friends. We swim or play volleyball. We have fun.

16 Complete the sentences.

topic sentence   detail sentence

A _____ tells us what the paragraph is about.

A _____ gives us more information.

17 Check (✓) the matching detail sentences.

Topic sentence: *Winter is my favorite time of year.*
1 It is cold and snowy in winter, but I like it.
2 It is not cold in summer.
3 My friends and I like to go sledding.
4 We usually wear hats and gloves in winter.
5 My sister's favorite season is spring.
6 We like to build snowmen in winter, too.

18 Write a topic sentence about your favorite season. Write three detail sentences under it.

Topic sentence: _____

Detail sentences: 1 _____
                   2 _____
                   3 _____

Phonics | sc, sw, sn, sl

I will learn to use the sounds *sc*, *sw*, *sn*, and *sl*.

19 Listen, read, and repeat.

1 sc   2 sw   3 sn   4 sl

20 Listen and find. Then say.

scarf   sweet   snail   sleep

21 Listen and blend the sounds.

1 s-c-ou-t   scout   2 s-n-a-ck   snack
3 s-w-i-m   swim   4 s-l-i-m   slim
5 s-n-ow   snow   6 s-w-a-n   swan
7 s-l-ow   slow   8 s-c-ar   scar

22 Read aloud. Then listen and chant.

A slow snail is eating a snack,
And a slim swan is swimming.

Values | Prepare for the weather.

I will learn to talk about preparing for the weather.

23 Look, listen, and point.

a   b   c

24 Look at **23**. Role-play with a partner.

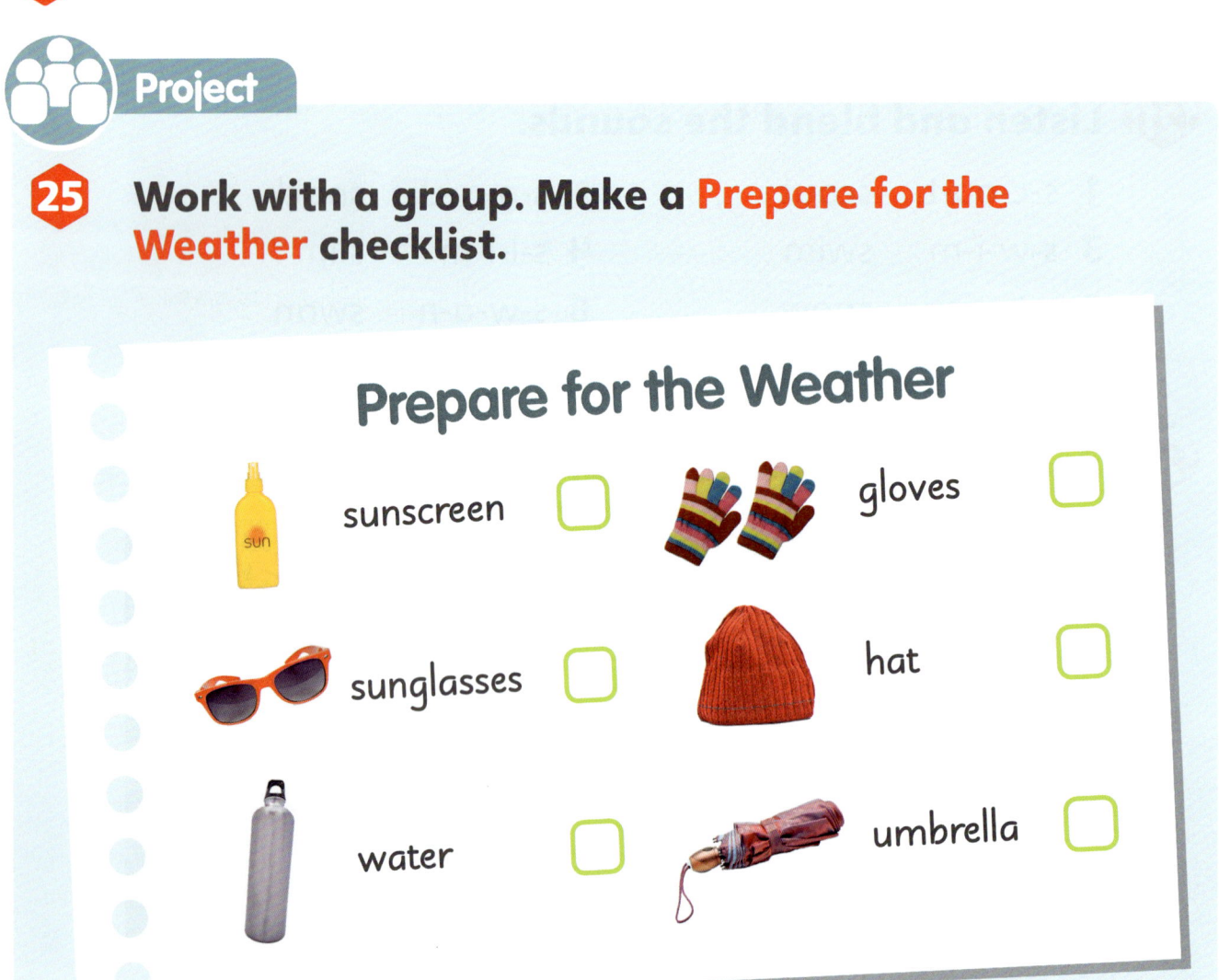

Project

25 Work with a group. Make a **Prepare for the Weather** checklist.

Prepare for the Weather

- sunscreen ☐
- gloves ☐
- sunglasses ☐
- hat ☐
- water ☐
- umbrella ☐

Review

26 Look at the weather reports. Ask and answer.

Barcelona, Spain

Yesterday	Today
Temperature: 33 °C	Temperature: 28 °C

Vancouver, Canada

Yesterday	Today
Temperature: 4 °C	Temperature: 12 °C

1 What/weather/Barcelona/yesterday?
Yesterday, it was _____.

2 What/weather/Barcelona/today?
Today, it's _____.

3 What/weather/Vancouver/yesterday?
_____

4 What/weather/Vancouver/today?
_____

27 Find the differences. Talk with a partner.

Picture 1

Picture 2

In Picture 1, the man wears summer clothes.

In Picture 2, the man wears winter clothes.

I Can

- use words for the weather and what clothes people wear in different types of weather.
- use *is* and *was* to ask and answer about the weather today and yesterday.
- talk about the weather around the world and what people wear.
- write detail sentences.

Unit 5

6 Smells Good!

Vocabulary

I will learn to name the five senses.

🎵 Song Time! 🎵

1 Listen, look, and say.

Senses

1. This music sounds beautiful.
2. This band sounds awful. 
3. This soup tastes horrible. 
4. This pie tastes delicious. 
5. This apple tastes sweet.
6. These flowers smell nice. 
7. My hair looks terrible. 
8. My sweater feels soft. 
9. These shoes feel tight. 

2 Play the silly sentences game.

Song

I will learn to ask and answer about the five senses.

3 **Listen and sing.** Why do the girls like Grandma's house?

Grandma's House

We love my grandma's house.
It always smells so nice.
It smells like ginger cookies,
Sweet, with a little spice!

We always do my favorite thing,
Baking ginger cookies.
They taste so nice and yummy,
We are both very lucky!

**Yummy smells and her smiling face.
We really love my grandma's place.**

Chorus

Grandma likes playing old songs
From when she was very young.
The music sounds so wonderful,
We have to sing along.

4 Match the pictures with the words. Then ask and answer about **1**.

feel
look
smell
sound
taste

1 2 3 4 5

This ice cream tastes delicious.

Number 4.

THINK BIG Can you think of other things you describe with these adjectives?
sweet   tight   beautiful   horrible

Unit 6 **69**

Story

I will read a story about the five senses.

🎧 Listen and read. What kind of soup does Luke try?

It Tastes Terrible!

1 Luke smells something bad coming from the kitchen.

- Ugh! What's that smell?
- What smell?

2 It is fish soup. Luke thinks it smells horrible.

- Ugh! This soup smells bad. It smells like fish.

3 Amy tries the soup.

- Try it, Amy! How does it taste?
- It tastes… OK.

4 Luke tries the soup.

- Really? It looks horrible. Let me try it.

70   Unit 6

5 Luke thinks the soup tastes awful.

"Yuck! It tastes terrible!"

6 Amy has a cold. That's why she can't taste the soup.

"Sorry, I have a cold... achoo! I can't smell or taste anything!"

6 **Put the sentences in order.**

a Amy thinks the soup tastes OK.
b Luke thinks the soup tastes terrible.
c Luke thinks the fish soup smells awful.
d Amy tries the soup.
e Luke tries the soup.
f Luke asks Amy to try the soup.

THINK BIG

Which senses do you use when you are...
a in a restaurant?   b at a soccer game?
c at school?
How do your senses make you aware of danger?

Unit 6 71

Language in Action

I will listen to a dialog about the five senses.

7 **Listen and read. Then say.**

Cindy: Hey, Mark. Do you want to hear my new song?
Mark: Uh… OK. Sure.
Cindy: *I don't want to run or play… I just want to sing all day…* So, how does it sound?
Mark: Um… it sounds… nice.
Cindy: Thanks! Do you want to hear more?
Mark: Uh… sorry, Cindy. I have to go. See you later!

8 **Look at 7. Role-play with a partner.**

9 **Listen and stick. Number the pictures.**

72 Unit 6

Grammar

I will learn to use *do* and *does* to ask and answer about the five senses.

| How **does** the apple pie **taste**? | It **tastes** delicious. |
| How **do** your new shoes **feel**? | They **feel** tight. |

10 **Circle the correct verb.**

1. **A:** How does the school band **sound / sounds**?
   B: They **sound / sounds** great. They practice every day.
2. **A:** How does my new shirt **look / looks**?
   B: It **look / looks** good. I like the color.
3. **A:** How does the sandwich **taste / tastes**?
   B: It **taste / tastes** awful. I don't like tomatoes!
4. **A:** How do these flowers **smell / smells**?
   B: They **smell / smells** nice.
5. **A:** How do your new gloves **feel / feels**?
   B: They **feel / feels** really warm.

11 **Complete the questions with do or does.**

1. How _____ that pizza taste?
2. How _____ the cookies smell?
3. How _____ my hair look today?
4. How _____ the shoes feel?
5. How _____ the guitar music sound?

12 **Look at 1. Ask and answer with a partner.**

How does the music sound?

It sounds beautiful.

Unit 6 73

Content Connection | Life Science

I will learn about how our senses keep us safe.

CONTENT WORDS
avoid   brain   danger
echo   information
senses   sound waves
taste buds   tongue

13 **Listen and read. Why are our senses important?**

Our Senses Keep Us Safe

Do you know what senses are for? Every minute of every day our senses get information and send it to our brain. We use this information to understand the world around us. With our senses we understand when food looks, smells, or tastes good and fresh, or when it's bad and rotten. We also feel something hot or sharp, or hear when danger is coming with our senses. Our senses are very important because they keep us safe.

Like people, animals use their senses to find food and avoid danger. But many animals' senses are very different from people's senses.

For example, we use our eyes to see, but bats can't see well. They have to use their ears. They make a sound and listen for an echo. They use the sound waves from the echo to 'see' how big something is and find it.

Snakes and lizards don't smell with their noses like us; they smell with their tongues! That's why their tongues are like a fork. The fork shape helps them understand where a smell is coming from.

Butterflies, on the other hand, don't taste with their tongues; they use their feet. They have tiny taste buds there. They help the butterfly understand what flower it is standing on. That's how they know they can eat it.

14 **Look at 13. Make sentences.**

1 Animals use their senses
2 Bats use sounds
3 Snakes use their tongues
4 Butterflies use their feet

a to taste things.
b to smell things.
c to find food and avoid danger.
d to understand the size of something.

THINK BIG Why do animals use their senses differently from people? Which sense is the most important? Why?

Culture Connection | Around the World

I will learn about smelly jobs in different countries.

CONTENT WORDS
awful   clean   fresh   smelly   stink   take care of   wet

15 🎧 **Listen and read. Which job smells best? Then match the jobs with the people.**

- **a** Baker
- **b** Zoo keeper
- **c** Garbage collector
- **d** Farmer

How Does Your Job Smell?

1 André Tyrode is from Lyon. He makes cakes and pastries every day. "Everything I make tastes and smells wonderful. It makes people want to share delicious treats together, and that makes me happy." Is there anything bad about his job? Well, he gets up at 5:00 a.m. every day!

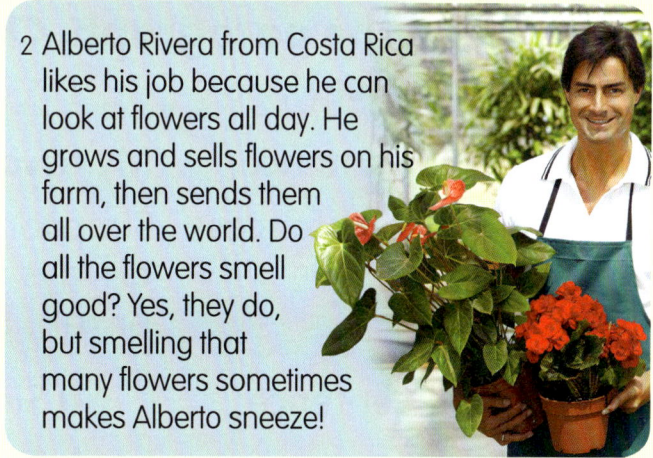

2 Alberto Rivera from Costa Rica likes his job because he can look at flowers all day. He grows and sells flowers on his farm, then sends them all over the world. Do all the flowers smell good? Yes, they do, but smelling that many flowers sometimes makes Alberto sneeze!

3 Candace Reilly is from Calgary, a city in Canada. She does a very important job. She picks trash and helps keep her city clean. Today, Calgary is the cleanest city in Canada! What does she say about a job like that? "My job doesn't smell great, in fact the trash really stinks, but I like making Calgary look, feel, and smell cleaner and better."

4 Sarah Ang takes care of Zelda, the Asian elephant at Singapore Zoo. It's one of the largest zoos in the world. "Sometimes Zelda smells, and I have to give her a bath. It's actually a great feeling when you take care of an animal like Zelda, but the smell is really awful." The bad thing is that when Sarah gives Zelda a bath, she has to take a bath, too.

THINK BIG Why do some people do jobs that aren't very nice?

Unit 6   75

Writing | Paragraph: Final Sentences

I will learn to write final sentences.

As you know, a paragraph begins with a **topic sentence**. It introduces the subject of the paragraph.
> I love tomatoes.

Detail sentences expand on your topic by giving details about it.
> Home-grown tomatoes taste delicious, and they are good for you.
> Fresh tomatoes right from the garden smell great.
> They look nice in a salad, too.

You end your paragraph with a **final sentence**. It expresses the same idea as your topic sentence but in a different way.
> Of all fruits and vegetables, tomatoes are my favorite.

16 **Read the paragraph. Check (✓) the best final sentence.**

Topic Sentence: My favorite toy is my teddy bear, Simpson.

Detail Sentences: Simpson is very old. He feels soft, and he always smells so nice. Simpson can't talk or run. But that's OK!

Final Sentence:
- [ ] a Simpson is just an old teddy bear.
- [ ] b I love Simpson more than any of my other toys.
- [ ] c Simpson doesn't do anything.

17 **Write a final sentence for this paragraph:**

Fall is my favorite season. The colorful leaves on the trees look so pretty. The air feels nice and cool. And fall smells great, like pumpkins and burning leaves.

Final Sentence: _____
_____

Phonics | fl, pl, gl, bl

I will learn to use the sounds *fl*, *pl*, *gl*, and *bl*.

18 **Listen, read, and repeat.**

1 fl   2 pl   3 gl   4 bl

19 **Listen and find. Then say.**

flip-**fl**ops   **pl**um   **gl**ass   **bl**ack

20 **Listen and blend the sounds.**

1 f-l-a-g   flag   2 p-l-a-n-t   plant
3 p-l-ay   play   4 f-l-y   fly
5 g-l-a-d   glad   6 g-l-ow   glow
7 b-l-o-ck   block   8 b-l-ow   blow

21 **Read aloud. Then listen and chant.**

It's summer.
Yellow plums,
Green plants.
Flip-flops,
Black shorts,
It's summer.
I'm glad!

Unit 6 77

Values | Try new things.

I will learn to talk about trying new things.

22 Look, listen, and point.

a b c

23 Practice with a partner. Talk about something new that you want to try.

My mom showed me how to make oatmeal cookies. Do you want to make them with me?

OK!

Project

24 Work with a group. Make a **Try New Things** flip chart.

Try New Things

bake cookies

78   Unit 6

Review

25 Complete the sentences with your own information.

1 My school lunch tastes _____.
2 When I sing, I sound _____.
3 My dog smells _____.
4 My mum looks _____.
5 My hat _____.
6 This apple _____.

26 Look at the pictures. Complete the questions.

1 How does the ice cream _____?
2 How does the rock band _____?
3 How does the man _____?
4 How does the stuffed animal _____?
5 How do the flowers _____?

I Can

- use words for how things look, feel, taste, smell, or sound.
- use verbs and adjectives to talk about the five senses.
- talk about the five senses.
- write final sentences.

Checkpoint | Units 4–6

How well do I know it? Can I use it?

1 **Think about it. Read and circle. Practice.**

I know this.

I don't know this.

I need more practice.

1. **Animals:** deer, owl, camel, lizard... — p. 44
2. **Habitats:** desert, ocean, rain forest... — p. 45
3. **Weather:** hot, cold, windy, rainy... — p. 56
4. **Describing:** awful, delicious, nice, sweet... — p. 68
5. What **can** penguins do?
   They **can** swim, but they **can't** fly. — p. 49
6. What **is** the weather like today?
   It**'s** hot and sunny. — p. 61
7. It **was** cold yesterday.
   We **were** freezing. — p. 61
8. How **does** the apple pie **taste**?
   It **tastes** delicious. — p. 73

I can do it!

Get ready.

A. Complete the dialog. Use the words from the box. Then listen and check.

> awful   cold   fly
> look   swim

Morgan: Look at those penguins!
Taylor: They ¹_____ cool!
Morgan: Yeah. I like penguins. Hey, look at this: "Penguins live in the snow and ice."
Taylor: That sounds ²_____!
Morgan: Yes, very cold. Listen. "They eat fish every day." Look. They're eating fish now!
Taylor: Yuck! That looks ³_____ to me!
Morgan: Well, the penguins like it.
Taylor: Hey, look. They're swimming.
Morgan: Yes, penguins can ⁴_____. But they can't ⁵_____.
Taylor: Wow. I'm learning a lot about penguins!

B. Practice the dialog in **A** with a partner. Then practice again. Talk about different animals.

C. Choose the words for you.
1 I **like** / **don't like** penguins.
2 Their food looks **delicious** / **terrible** to me.
3 Their home looks **warm** / **cold** to me.

Checkpoint Units 4–6   81

Checkpoint | Units 4–6

3 **Get set.**

STEP 1 Look and read. Find out information about an animal.

STEP 2 Cut out the book outline on page 135. Fold it to make a book.

STEP 3 Write in your own animal information book. Now you're ready to **Go**!

4 **Go!**

A. Swap books with five classmates. Write notes about their books in your notebook.

Classmate	Animal	Comment
Carla	lizards	great

B. Tell the class about some of your classmates' books.

> Elena's book was about sharks. Sharks are amazing!

5 **Write about yourself in your notebook.**

- What was the weather like today?
- What was the weather like yesterday?
- My classroom feels...
- My favorite animal is...
- I like this animal because...

All About Me

How well do I know it now?

6 **Think about it.**

A. Go to page 80. Look and circle again.

B. Check (✔).

☐ I can start the next unit.

☐ I can ask my teacher for help and then start the next unit.

☐ I can practice and then start the next unit.

7 **Rate this Checkpoint. Color.**

hard   OK   easy   not fun   OK   fun

7 Fabulous Food!

Vocabulary

I will learn to name foods.

🎵 Song Time! 🎵

1 Listen, look, and say.

At *Your Way Café* you decide what to put in your sandwich or on your pizza. There are so many things to choose from. Which will you choose?

1 Super Sandwiches!

1. bread
2. cucumbers
3. turkey
4. mustard
5. lettuce

2 Pizza Perfection!

6. green peppers
7. mushrooms
8. tomato sauce
9. olives
10. onions

2 Play the acting game.

84 Unit 7

Song

I will learn to ask and answer about food.

3 **Listen and sing. What do they eat?**

I'm Hungry!

Hi, Mom, I'm home from school.
I'm really hungry now.
I'd like to make a sandwich,
Can you show me how?

**I am home from my school day.
I'd like a sandwich. Is that OK?**

Are there any olives?
Here are some on the shelf.
Is there any tomato sauce?
I see it for myself.

Chorus

There's just one problem, Mom:
There isn't any bread!
But I have a great idea:
Let's have pizza instead!

Chorus

4 **Look at 1. Ask and answer.**

What do you like in your sandwiches?

I like turkey and lettuce.

THINK BIG What do you like on pizzas and in sandwiches?

Unit 7　85

Story

I will read a story about food.

🎧 5 Listen and read. What are Luke and Amy making?

A Surprise for Mom

1 Luke and Amy are making dinner for their mom. It's a surprise.

- Are there any tomatoes for the pizza?
- I can't see any, but there's some cheese.

2 They need toppings for their pizza.

- Are there any onions?
- No, there aren't. But there's a green pepper.

3 Amy and Luke taste some of the pizza toppings.

- This cheese is yummy.
- Mmm. These olives taste delicious, too!

4 They look in the fridge again. What can they use?

- Oh, no! There isn't any more cheese.
- And there aren't any more olives. Oops.

86 Unit 7

> Hmm. Is there any bread over there?

> Look! There's some turkey.

> Hi, Mom!

> Mom... Can we go out for dinner, please?

5 Amy and Luke look for more food.

6 There's a surprise for Mom in the kitchen, but it isn't dinner!

6 Read and say true or false.

1 Amy and Luke want to make breakfast for their mother.
2 There aren't any onions for the pizza.
3 Amy and Luke eat all the cheese and olives.
4 There isn't any turkey.
5 There isn't a surprise for Mom.

THINK BIG
Do you help your mom?
How could you help your family?

Language in Action

I will listen to a dialog about food.

7 **Listen and read. Then say.**

Felipa: What are you making, Mom?
Mom: I'm making some salsa.
Felipa: That sounds great!
Mom: I have some tomatoes, some chili peppers… Are there any onions over there?
Felipa: Yes. Here they are.
Mom: Thanks.
Felipa: Mmm. That looks delicious, Mom. But there's a little problem.
Mom: What?
Felipa: Now we have salsa, but there aren't any chips!

8 **Look at 7. Role-play with a partner.**

9 **Listen and stick. Number the pictures.**

Grammar

I will learn to use *some* and *any* to ask and answer about food.

| Is there **any** pizza? | Yes, there is **some** pizza. | Are there **any** onions? | Yes, there are **some** onions. |
| Is there **any** lettuce? | No, there isn't **any** lettuce. | Are there **any** eggs? | No, there aren't **any** eggs. |

10 **Look at the chart above. Circle the correct word.**

1 There are **some** / **any** apples on the table.
2 There aren't **some** / **any** eggs in the refrigerator.
3 There isn't **some** / **any** milk in the carton.
4 There is **some** / **any** mustard in the jar.
5 There aren't **some** / **any** onions in this stew.

11 **Look at 1. Write questions and answers.**

1 Is there any bread?
   _____

2 Are there any onions?
   _____

3 _____
   No, there isn't any cake.

4 _____
   No, there aren't any bananas.

5 _____
   Yes, there are some cucumbers.

Content Connection | Science

I will learn about vitamins.

CONTENT WORDS

blood   bone   brain   energy   healthy   iron   muscle   skin   teeth   vitamin

12 Listen and read. How many different fruit and vegetables should we eat each day?

The Vitamin Alphabet

Vitamins help our bodies grow strong and stay healthy. But which foods do we get our vitamins from? And why do we need them?

Vitamin A: There's a lot of Vitamin A in orange and yellow fruits like carrots or mangoes, but you can also find some in milk and the yellow part of eggs. Vitamin A helps your eyes and skin stay healthy.

Vitamin D: Milk and eggs also have Vitamin D in them, and so does fish. When we sit in the sun, our body makes a lot of it naturally. This vitamin is very important for strong bones.

Vitamin E: This, on the other hand, helps keep our blood healthy. You can get Vitamin E when you eat nuts and green vegetables.

Vitamin B: There are many different kinds of Vitamin B. Some help give us energy to move our muscles. Others help make blood. We get the different kinds of Vitamin B from different kinds of food. These include potatoes, bananas, bread, rice, pasta, chicken, fish, cheese, eggs, and green peppers.

Vitamin C: Vitamin C is good for our bones, teeth, and even our brains. We get this vitamin from oranges, peppers, tomatoes, and potatoes. Vitamin C also helps us keep other important substances, iron for example, in our body.

We should eat a good variety of fruit and vegetables – at least five a day. But we can eat some 'bad' things too. For example, there are three B vitamins in a good bar of dark chocolate!

13 Work with a partner. Read and say true or false.

1. You can only find vitamins in fruit and vegetables.
2. There aren't any vitamins in chocolate.
3. There's a lot of vitamin A in orange fruits and vegetables.

THINK BIG

Which vitamins do the following people need and why?
a a soccer player   b a pilot

Culture Connection | Around the World

I will learn about meals around the world.

🎧 **14** **Listen and fill in the gaps. Which of these foods would you like to try?**

CONTENT WORDS
bake boil dough
fry oil soup
pickled spicy steam

Dumplings: A Global Food

Food can be very different from culture to culture. But there is a type of food that almost every culture shares: the dumpling. What is a dumpling? A dumpling is a piece of dough. You put fillings inside, and then boil, _____, bake, or fry them. Here are some of the most popular dumplings around the world.

Mandu

This dumpling comes from South Korea. Fillings for mandu can be meat and vegetables, or often you can find kimchi mandu – a dumpling filled with kimchi, a kind of _____, pickled cabbage.

Empanada

Across Central and South America, it is easy to find these dumplings. They are filled with ground beef, chicken, or other meats. Then they are fried in hot _____. They are bigger than many other dumplings.

Pierogi

This dumpling is easy to find across Eastern Europe, but many people say they are from Poland. Fillings for this type of dumpling can be potatoes, cheese, meat, or sauerkraut – a salty, pickled cabbage. You can _____ them in butter and onions. Delicious!

Xiao Long Bao

Shanghai, China, is known for its famous _____ dumplings. These dumplings are filled with meat and served in a hot, delicious soup. The soup goes inside the dumplings and gives them a special flavor.

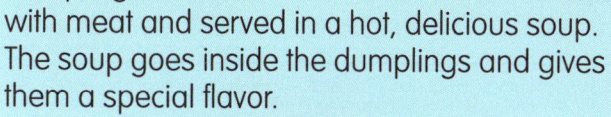

Ravioli

Most people call this a type of pasta, but it is also a dumpling. Ravioli are well known in Italian cooking. They can be filled with many different things: meat, cheese, vegetables, or sometimes all three. You usually _____ the ravoli and serve them with sauce and cheese.

THINK BIG What types of dumplings do you like? When do you eat them?

Unit 7 91

Writing | Paragraphs

I will learn to write paragraphs.

15 Listen and read.

title → My Favorite Breakfast
by Laura Brown

topic sentence → I like many foods for breakfast, but I have my favorite breakfast every Sunday morning.

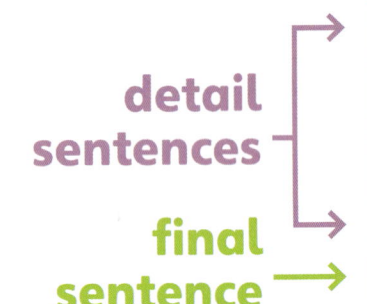

detail sentences → I start with some orange slices, cold from the refrigerator. Then my mother makes two fluffy pancakes for me. I put butter on them, and then I put warm maple syrup on top. The pancakes are delicious with a glass of cold milk.

final sentence → My favorite breakfast makes Sundays special.

16 Listen to Laura's paragraph again. Work with a partner. Take turns and read each part of the paragraph aloud.

17 Write about your favorite meal.

_____
(title)

_____
_____
_____
_____
_____
_____

Writing Steps

1. Think about your favorite meal.
2. Write a title.
3. Write a topic sentence.
4. Add detail sentences to give more information.
5. Write a final sentence.

Phonics | br, cr, dr, fr, gr, pr, tr

I will learn to use the sounds *br*, *cr*, *dr*, *fr*, *gr*, *pr*, and *tr*.

18 Listen, read, and repeat.

1. br 2. cr 3. dr 4. fr 5. gr 6. pr 7. tr

19 Listen and find. Then say.

bread **cr**eam  **dr**eam  **fr**og

grass  **pr**ize  **tr**ain

20 Listen and blend the sounds.

1. d-r-i-ve — drive
2. g-r-ee-n — green
3. b-r-ow-n — brown
4. p-r-i-n-ce — prince
5. c-r-y — cry
6. t-r-o-ll — troll
7. f-r-o-m — from
8. b-r-i-ck — brick

21 Read aloud. Then listen and chant.

Every night,
I dream
About a prince
And a troll,
And a green frog!
In my dream,
They eat bread
With cream.

Unit 7

Values | Try different foods.

I will learn to talk about food from other countries.

22 Listen. Look at the poster. Which dish looks good to you? Discuss with a partner.

Potatoes in Peru

Peruvians love potatoes. Peru grows more than 2,300 types of potatoes. There are many different shapes, sizes, and colors!

Potatoes grow very well in the cool weather, high in the Andes Mountains.

The most famous dish is *papa a la huancaína* – potatoes in a spicy cheese sauce.

Another is *papa rellena*, or stuffed potato. This dish has meat, onions, and eggs stuffed inside a potato.

I want to try the stuffed potato. It looks delicious!

Project

23 Make a poster about the food in a country other than your own.

1. Learn about the typical foods in that country.
2. Cut out pictures of the foods.
3. Label the pictures.
4. Share your poster with the class.

CHINA — noodles, dumplings, fried rice

94   Unit 7

Review

24 Make up a sandwich with five items.

My sandwich has bread and...

1. _____
2. _____
3. _____
4. _____
5. _____

Ask other classmates about their sandwiches.

Are there any mushrooms in your sandwich?

No, there aren't.

Make notes about your classmates' sandwiches. Try to find two people with the same sandwich.

Student 1: _____	Student 2: _____	Student 3: _____
1	1	1
2	2	2
3	3	3

I Can

- use food words.
- use *some* and *any* to ask and answer questions about food.
- ask and answer about food.
- write a paragraph about my favorite meal.

Unit 7 **95**

8 Healthy Living

Vocabulary

I will learn to name healthy and unhealthy habits.

🎵 Song Time! 🎵

1. Listen, look, and say.

How do you feel today? Find out how healthy Sally and Zach are, then ask yourself!

1. Did she have a big breakfast?
2. Did she get 10 hours of sleep last night?
3. Did she drink lots of water?
4. Did she ride her bike?
5. Did he eat breakfast?
6. Did he get any exercise?
7. Did he have a healthy lunch?
8. Did he get enough sleep?

2. Play the acting game.

96 Unit 8

Song

I will learn to ask and answer about healthy and unhealthy habits.

3 Listen and sing. What is good for Zach?

Live Right!

"Did you eat breakfast?" asks Mom,
"You don't look good to me.
Did you get enough sleep?" asks Mom,
"Did you watch too much TV?"

**Enough sleep. Good food.
Be healthy. Live right!
Enough sleep. Good food.
Be healthy. Live right!**

"Did you ride your bike?" asks Mom,
"You know it's good for you.
Did you get any exercise?
You know it's good to do!"

Chorus

I feel awful today.

4 Look at 1. Ask and answer.

Did he eat breakfast?

No, he didn't.

Did she ride her bike?

Yes, she did.

THINK BIG Which child in 1 are you like? Explain why.

Unit 8   97

Story

I will read a story about healthy and unhealthy habits.

🎧 5 Listen and read. Did Amy eat a healthy dinner?

An Unhealthy Dinner

1 Amy's dad wants her to be healthy.

- How was the party?
- Uh...
- Did you eat healthy food?
- Kind of...

2 Amy likes unhealthy food.

- Well, did you eat any vegetables?
- Yes, I did. I ate two burgers. They had onions and ketchup on them. Onions and tomatoes are vegetables!

3 Amy likes fries, but fried food isn't very healthy.

- Yes, I guess so.
- And I ate lots of fries. Fries are potatoes. They are vegetables, aren't they?

4 Amy likes soda.

- Did you drink any water?
- No, I didn't. I drank a large soda.

98 Unit 8

5 What? That dinner wasn't healthy!

Well, yes, but there's a lot of sugar in soda.

But soda has water in it!

Amy knows her dinner wasn't really healthy. She didn't eat many vegetables.

6 Oh... my stomach feels funny!

Now Amy doesn't feel well. She needs to eat healthy food.

6 Read and circle.

1 Amy had dinner at **a party** / **home**.
2 Amy likes **healthy** / **unhealthy** food.
3 Fries are fried **potatoes** / **onions**.
4 Fried food is **good** / **bad** for you.
5 Soda has a lot of **fruit** / **sugar** in it.
6 Amy's dad **is** / **isn't** happy about Amy's dinner.

THINK BIG What do you like to eat for dinner? Why?

Language in Action

I will listen to a dialog about healthy and unhealthy habits.

7 **Listen and read. Then say.**

Tomas: Hi, Mariela. How are you?
Mariela: I feel great today! I got lots of sleep. I ate a good breakfast. How about you?
Tomas: I don't feel good today.
Mariela: Why? Did you eat breakfast?
Tomas: Yes, I did. I ate three donuts.
Mariela: Three donuts! That's why you feel bad!

8 **Look at 7. Role-play with a partner.**

9 **Listen and stick.**

Peggy — Saturday — Sunday

Carlos — Saturday — Sunday

100 Unit 8

Grammar

I will learn to use *did* and *didn't* to ask and answer about healthy and unhealthy habits.

| **Did** you/he/she/they **get** enough sleep yesterday? | Yes, I/he/she/they **did**. | No, I/he/she/they **didn't**. |

10 **Complete the dialogs. Use did or didn't.**

1. **A:** Good morning, Katia. _____ you eat breakfast?
   B: Yes, I _____.
2. **A:** _____ Ted take a shower this morning?
   B: No, he _____.
3. **A:** _____ the lacrosse team get enough sleep before the game?
   B: No, they _____.

11 **Look at the chart. Write questions and answers about Becca.**

Becca's Habits	Mon	Tue	Wed	Thu	Fri
1 drink lots of water	✓		✓	✓	
2 get enough exercise	✓	✓	✓		

1 (exercise/Monday) _____

   Yes, _____

2 (drink water/Tuesday) _____

   No, _____

12 **Talk about your habits. Ask and answer with a partner.**

Did you get enough exercise today?

No, I didn't.

Unit 8

Content Connection | Science

I will learn about calories.

CONTENT WORDS
active   activities   body   burn
calorie   measure   put on weight

13 Listen and read. What activities are good or bad for your body?

What Is a Calorie?

What are calories? Are they important?
A calorie is a measure of the energy you get from food. Some foods are high in calories, and other foods aren't. Your body needs a certain number of calories to do all the things you do every day. But if you eat more calories than your body needs, you put on too much weight. Lots of activity and exercise burns a lot of calories. Very little activity or exercise doesn't burn a lot of calories.

Why is being active good for us?
It helps our hearts stay healthy. It makes our bones strong, and it creates muscles. Being active is really important for young and old people. Activities that use lots of energy are best. Dancing is really good for your body. Riding a bike and swimming are also good for your body. But watching TV or playing video games are bad for your health if you do them too much. That's because you sit in the same place to do them.

14 Complete the chart. Use the activities from the box. Then add more activities.

dancing   playing a sport   playing video games
riding my bike to school   watching TV

Good for your body	Bad for your body

THINK BIG How much exercise do you do? How much time do you spend in front of the TV?

102   Unit 8

Culture Connection | Around the World

I will learn about sports around the world.

CONTENT WORDS
contest   net   puck   race   regatta   team

15 Listen and read. Where do these sports come from?

Strange Sports

Almost everyone knows about soccer, baseball, and basketball. But do you know anything about octopush, footvolley, or pumpkin regattas? Read about these strange sports!

Octopush
Octopush comes from England, but people now play it all over the world. Octopush is like hockey, but people play it under water. Players use a small stick. They try to push a puck into a net to score points for their team.

Pumpkin Regatta
Each fall, in parts of the United States and Canada, people join in a contest called a pumpkin regatta. It is like a boat race, but the players do not race in boats. They race in giant, hollowed out pumpkins! These pumpkins weigh more than 450 kilograms (1,000 pounds). After the race, there's a pumpkin pie-eating contest.

Footvolley
Footvolley is a sport from Brazil. Footvolley is like volleyball, but the players use a soccer ball. Players have to pass the ball to the other team over a high net. They cannot touch the ball with their hands. People play footvolley on the beach. It is very exciting but very difficult!

16 Which sport do you want to try? Talk with a partner.

THINK BIG Why did these sports start in these places? Can you do these sports in other countries?

Unit 8   103

Writing | Combining Sentences with *and*, *but*, *or*

I will learn to combine sentences with *and*, *but*, *or*.

Use **and**, **but**, and **or** to combine two simple sentences into one compound sentence.
 I went to bed at 9:00. I woke up at 7:00.
  → I went to bed at 9:00, **and** I woke up at 7:00.
 Dad ate oatmeal. Mom didn't eat breakfast.
  → Dad ate oatmeal, **but** Mom didn't eat breakfast.
 We can walk to the store. We can take the bus.
  → We can walk to the store, **or** we can take the bus.

17 Circle the words *and*, *but*, and *or* in the paragraph.

I don't like to play sports, but I need to get exercise. I like walking, and I walk to school every day. My dad goes hiking on the weekend, or he goes to the gym. I like to go to the gym with him. He lifts weights, and I walk on the treadmill. For a treat afterward, we go out for smoothies, or we make tacos at home. Dad makes the best tacos, but Mom's cooking is good, too.

18 Join the simple sentences to make compound sentences. Use the word in parentheses.

1 My sister plays soccer. My brother plays baseball. (and)
 _____

2 My dad works at a hospital. He isn't a doctor. (but)
 _____

3 We can eat chicken for dinner. We can try the new restaurant. (or)
 _____

4 Freddie can run two miles. He doesn't run fast. (but)
 _____

Phonics | *all, au, aw*

I will learn to use the sounds *all*, *au*, and *aw*.

19 Listen, read, and repeat.

1 **all**   2 **au**   3 **aw**

20 Listen and find. Then say.

b**all**   h**aul**   dr**aw**

21 Listen and blend the sounds.

1 s-m-all   small
2 c-all   call
3 t-all   tall
4 y-aw-n   yawn
5 c-l-aw   claw
6 w-all   wall
7 l-aw   law
8 P-aul   Paul

22 Read aloud. Then listen and chant.

I'm Paul, I'm bored.
Yawn, yawn.
Let's play, let's play
With a ball,
Let's draw, let's draw
A wall.

Unit 8

Values | Get exercise.

I will learn to talk about exercise.

23 🎧 159 **Look and listen. Point to and say the healthy activities.**

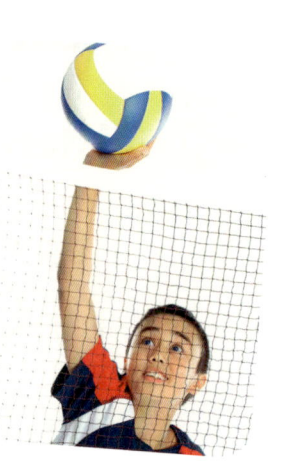

a b c d

24 Work with a partner. Tell your partner to do healthy things.

Don't watch TV. Go outside and play soccer!

Ride your bike at a park or in your neighborhood. It's fun, and it's good for you.

Project

25 Work with a group. Think of a new game you can play outside. Write down the rules. Teach the rest of the class your new game.

Review

26 **Circle the correct verb.**

1 Lenny is tired. He didn't **get / got** enough sleep last night.
2 I feel sick. I didn't **eat / eating** a healthy breakfast.
3 Did they drink lots of water today? No, they **did / didn't**.
4 Did they **ride / rode** their bikes yesterday? Yes, it was fun.

27 **Do a survey of your classmates. Add two of your own questions. Ask and answer.**

1 eat/healthy/food?
2 get/sleep/last night?
3 get/exercise/last week?
4 brush/teeth/this morning?
5 ride/bike/on the weekend?
6 drink/a lot of/water/today?
7 _____
8 _____

Did you get enough sleep last night?

Yes, I did.

I Can

- use words for healthy and unhealthy habits.
- use *did* and *didn't* to ask questions about healthy and unhealthy habits.
- ask and answer about healthy and unhealthy habits.
- combine sentences with *and*, *but*, and *or*.

Unit 8   107

9 School Trips!

Vocabulary

I will learn to name places to visit.

🎵 Song Time! 🎵

1 Listen, look, and say.

Top 8 places to visit!

1. museum
2. dairy farm 
3. art gallery 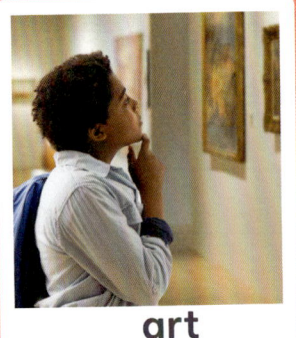
4. national park 
5. theater 
6. zoo 
7. concert hall 
8. aquarium 

2 Play the description game.

Song

I will learn to ask and answer about school trips.

3 Listen and sing. Where did she go?

Learning Out of School

I like going on school trips,
Learning out of school.
We go to lots of places.
They're interesting and cool!

Aquarium, theater, concert hall, and zoo,
We saw some great things.
There was lots to do!

**School trips. School trips.
They're a lot of fun.
School trips. School trips.
Let's go on one!**

Where did you go?
What did you see?
We went to the zoo, we saw a play,
We had a great time!

Chorus

4 Look at 1. Ask and answer.

It was a cloudy day.

Yes, I did.

Did you go to a national park?

THINK BIG Why is it good to go on school trips?

Story

I will read a story about a school trip.

5. Listen and read. Did Luke enjoy the trip?

A Cool Trip

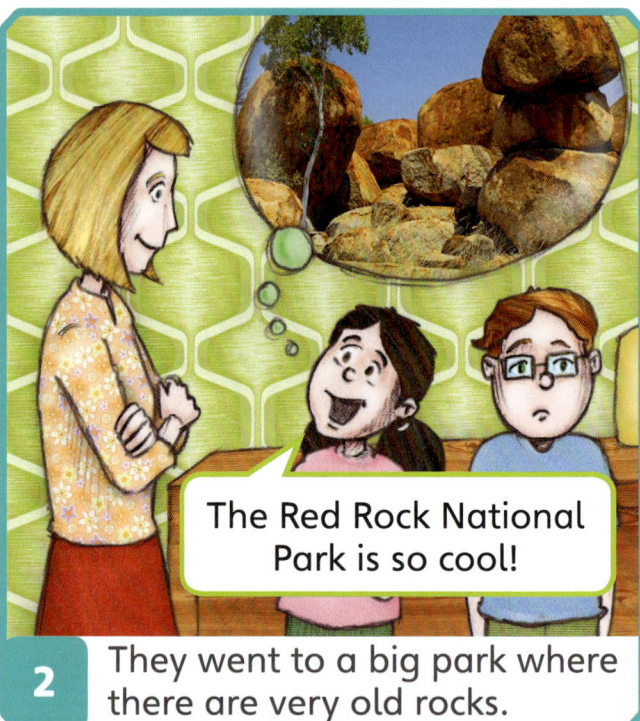

1 Amy and Luke went on a trip today.

- Hi, Luke. Hi, Amy. How was your trip today?
- It was OK.
- It was fantastic!

2 They went to a big park where there are very old rocks.

- The Red Rock National Park is so cool!

3 Their guide told them a lot of things about the rocks in the park.

- What did you do there?
- We learned about rocks. There are so many kinds of rocks, Mom!

4 Amy liked the park.

- So did you like it?
- Yes, I did. It was really interesting.

5 Yes, Amy liked it, but I didn't. We walked… and walked… and walked…

Luke didn't like the trip. He didn't like walking a lot.

6 Oh, Luke! It was fun! And I got you a present from the gift shop!

Did you? What?

A rock!

Luke doesn't want to see another rock!

6 Read and answer.

1 Where did Luke and Amy go on their trip?
2 What did they learn about?
3 Did Amy like the trip? Why/Why not?
4 Did Luke enjoy the trip? Why/Why not?
5 What did Amy get for Luke in the gift shop?

THINK BIG What national parks are there in your country? Why do we have national parks?

Language in Action

I will listen to a dialog about school trips.

7. Listen and read. Then say.

Grandpa: What did you do at school today?
Susana: We went on a field trip.
Grandpa: Oh, that's nice. Where did you go?
Susana: We went to the aquarium.
Grandpa: What did you do there?
Susana: We got to pet baby sharks.
Grandpa: Did you like the aquarium?
Susana: Yes, I liked it a lot. It was really cool!

8. Look at 7. Role-play with a partner.

9. Listen and stick.

Grammar

I will learn to use *did* to ask and answer about where people went and what they did.

Where **did** you/he/she/they go?	I/He/She/They **went** to an art gallery.	
What **did** you/he/she/they **see**?	I/He/She/They **saw** a play.	
Did you/he/she/they **like** it?	Yes, I/he/she/they **liked** it.	No, I/he/she/they **didn't like** it.

10 Complete the dialog.

A: Where ¹_____ you go yesterday?
B: I ²_____ to see a movie.
A: What ³_____ you see?
B: I ⁴_____ that new horror movie.
A: ⁵_____ you like it?
B: No, I ⁶_____ it. It was too scary.

11 Read and match. Make sentences.

1 We went to a dairy farm   a the play.
2 What did you see   b go yesterday?
3 She didn't like   c like rock music.
4 Where did you   d to learn about milking cows.
5 I don't really   e at the National Museum?

12 Work with a partner. Ask and answer questions. Use the words from the box.

last weekend   last year   yesterday

Where did you go yesterday?

I went to an art gallery.

Unit 9

Content Connection | Art

I will learn about paintings.

CONTENT WORDS
artist colorful happy
impressionist painter
sad strange

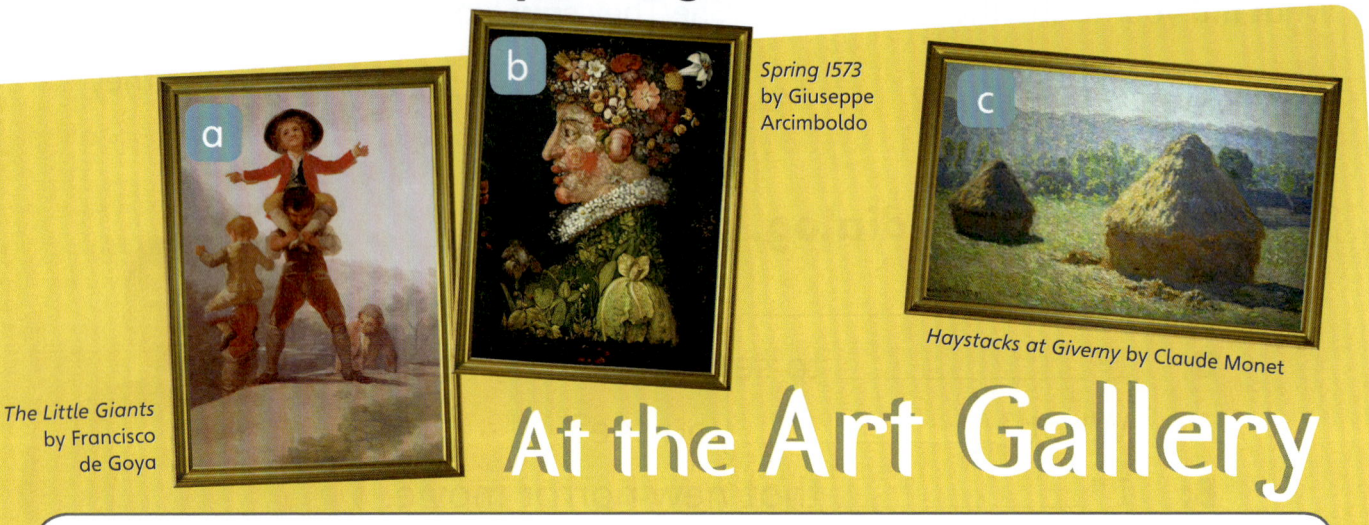

13 **Listen and read. Why does Amy like her favorite painting?**

Spring 1573 by Giuseppe Arcimboldo

Haystacks at Giverny by Claude Monet

The Little Giants by Francisco de Goya

At the Art Gallery

@Amylovesart Last week, I went to the National Gallery with my mom. Was it boring? No way! This was my favorite painting. An Italian artist painted it in the 16th century. It looks like a face, doesn't it? It is, but it's also lots of other things. Every part of the face and body is a different spring fruit, vegetable, or flower. I like this picture because it's pretty, colorful, and smart. It shows humans and nature.

@ConchiConchi I love this painting from the Prado Museum in Madrid. There are children in it. The young children look happy, but the older children look a little tired. Mom says the artist painted it in the 19th century just before he stopped hearing. He went deaf. That's really sad. I think the painter became an artist for the king of Spain.

@MattieMonstreParis A French impressionist painter painted the original, and it's in the Musée d'Orsay in Paris. Anyway, this reminds me of summer. It's on a farm, probably. My grandmother says this is one of the painter's best paintings. He painted another twenty paintings like this with different colors. That's a little strange, isn't it?

@Amylovesart Wow! So many great paintings in museums all over the world. I'd like to see them one day!

14 **Look at the passage and match the paragraphs with the pictures.**

THINK BIG What do you like to see most in paintings; people, animals, or nature? Why?

Culture Connection | Around the World

I will learn about theater around the world.

CONTENT WORDS
dramatic flamenco open-air theater
performance play popular
puppet show stage

15 Listen and read. Where did the first theater open?

The World Stage

Today around the world, different countries have different types of stage performances that were popular in the past and are popular today.

There were theaters in Greece more than 2,000 years ago. Greek plays were funny or sad, but all of them taught important lessons about life. In those times, all the actors were men or boys, and there was a chorus with people singing. Greek plays are still popular today, and every summer people enjoy watching them in open-air theaters.

In Spain, people love watching performances of flamenco dancing and music. Flamenco comes from Southern Spain. It started hundreds of years ago when people moved to Spain from the East. Usually there's a guitar, and men and women dance. 'Palmeros' clap in a special way with the dancers. Flamenco music and dance are very dramatic.

In Vietnam, people enjoy watching an interesting kind of theater called Mua Roi Nuoc. There aren't any actors – only puppets. The puppets are on a stage filled with water. People from the Red River Delta began doing Mua Roi Nuoc puppet shows in the 11th century, but people still watch performances today. They're magical.

16 Work with a partner and guess. When did these things happen? Match the sections to make sentences.

1	The first movie theater opened	in Vienna, Austria,	in 1765. They called it an animal menagerie.
2	The first zoo opened	in New Orleans,	in 1896. All the movies were silent.
3	Families bought their first TVs	in the U.S.,	in 1945. They cost $100.

THINK BIG Which do you prefer watching; dance, theater, or movies? Why?

Unit 9 115

Writing | Sentence: Subjects, verbs, and objects

I will learn to write sentences with a subject, verb, and object.

> Sentences have **subjects**, **verbs**, and **objects**.
> They appear in this order:
>   We had fun.
>   They didn't see a show.
>   Did you see a sea lion show?

17 Find the **subjects**, **verbs**, and **objects**.
  1 Did she visit a dairy farm?
  2 They didn't see any scary paintings.
  3 I learned about rocks.
  4 Did you see a movie?

18 Circle the correct verb.
  1 I **doesn't** / **don't** like peas.
  2 Meg **go** / **goes** to art class.
  3 They **is** / **are** my friends.
  4 We **doesn't** / **don't** play soccer.
  5 You **isn't** / **aren't** hungry.

19 Put the words in order to make detail sentences.
  1 went | We | to the National Gallery.
  2 old and new paintings. | saw | I
  3 love | I | painting and listening to guides.
  4 Our | class | famous artists. | learned about

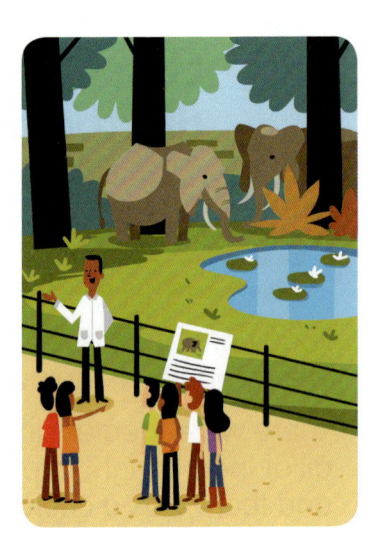

116 Unit 9

Phonics | *nt, ld, nd, st*

I will learn to use the sounds *nt*, *ld*, *nd*, and *st*.

20 Listen, read, and repeat.

1. nt
2. ld
3. nd
4. st

21 Listen and find. Then say.

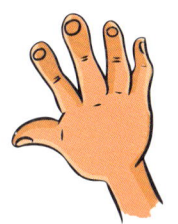

te**nt**   chi**ld**   ha**nd**   ne**st**

22 Listen and blend the sounds.

1. p-l-a-n-t   plant
2. o-l-d   old
3. c-o-l-d   cold
4. b-a-n-d   band
5. s-a-n-d   sand
6. a-n-t   ant
7. ch-e-s-t   chest
8. f-a-s-t   fast

23 Read aloud. Then listen and chant.

An old, cold band
Playing in the sand.
A fast ant
Playing in a tent.

Unit 9 **117**

Values | Recognize your talents.

I will learn to talk about my talents.

24 **Complete the chart using the words from the box.**

basketball   dance   drawing   English   math
painting   science   soccer   swimming

Sports	Arts	School Subjects
_____	_____	_____
_____	_____	_____
_____	_____	_____

25 **Work with a partner. Talk about your talents.**

Do you like math?

No, I don't. But I like art! I'm good at painting.

Project

26 Have a **Talent Show**. Share your talent with the class.

Class Talent Show

118 Unit 9

Review

27 Look and say the places.

1   2   3   4

28 Complete the dialog. Then role-play with a partner.

A: Hey! How are you, Claudia?
B: I'm fine, Dad.
A: Where did you ¹_____ today?
B: I ²_____ on a school trip to the zoo.
A: Cool! What ³_____ you ⁴_____?
B: We saw a ⁵_____ and a giraffe.
A: That sounds fun. Did you ⁶_____ it?
B: Yes. I ⁷_____. It ⁸_____ really fun!

29 Make up your own field trip. Then talk with a partner.

1 Where did you go?
2 What did you see?
3 Did you like it? Why or why not?

> We went to a toy museum. We saw some very old toys. Some of them were a hundred years old! We liked it a lot.

I Can

- use words for places to visit on a school trip.
- ask and answer questions using the past simple.
- talk about school trips.
- write sentences with a subject, verb, and object.

Unit 9 119

Checkpoint | Units 7–9

How well do I know it? Can I use it?

1 **Think about it. Read and circle. Practice.**

😊 ← I know this.   😠 ← I don't know this.

😐 ← I need more practice.

1	**Food:** bread, mustard, onions, turkey...	😊 😐 😠	p. 84
2	**Healthy habits:** ate breakfast, drank water, got enough sleep, rode my bike...	😊 😐 😠	p. 96
3	**School trip places:** aquarium, museum, national park, theater...	😊 😐 😠	p. 108
4	Is there **any** pizza? Yes, there is **some** pizza.	😊 😐 😠	p. 89
5	**Did** you **get** enough sleep? Yes, I **did**.	😊 😐 😠	p. 101
6	Where **did** they go? They **went** to the museum. **Did** they **like** it? Yes, they **liked** it.	😊 😐 😠	p. 113

120 Checkpoint Units 7–9

I can do it!

🎧 **Get ready.**

A. Complete the dialog with Kelly's answers. Then listen and check.

Kelly: Hello?
Dad: Hi, Kelly. It's Dad.
Kelly: Oh, hi, Dad!
Dad: How is New York City?
Kelly: 1 _____
Dad: What did you do yesterday?
Kelly: 2 _____
Dad: That sounds fun. Did you like it?
Kelly: 3 _____
Dad: Great. So, when is your soccer game?
Kelly: 4 _____
Dad: I see. Did you get enough sleep last night?
Kelly: 5 _____
Dad: That's good. Did you eat breakfast this morning?
Kelly: 6 _____
Dad: That sounds delicious! Well, good luck today. Call me after your game.
Kelly: OK, Dad. Talk to you later.
Dad: Bye.

Kelly's answers
a   Yes, Dad. I ate a big pancake.
b   Yes, it was great! We saw a lot of interesting paintings.
c   Yes, I went to bed at 7:00 last night.
d   We went to the Museum of Modern Art.
e   It's today. It starts at 2:00.
f   It's really cool. We arrived yesterday afternoon.

B. Practice the dialog in **A** with a partner. Make up your own answers.

Checkpoint Units 7–9

Checkpoint | Units 7–9

3 Get set.

STEP 1 Cut out the cards on page **137**.

STEP 2 Read Dialog 1 below. Then place the cards in order to create Dialog 2.

STEP 3 Look at the pictures below. Choose the picture that illustrates each dialog. Now you're ready to **Go**!

4 Go!

A. With a partner, practice Dialog 1. Change parts and practice again.

A: Where did you go yesterday?
B: We went to a big art gallery.
A: What did you do there?
B: We looked at some paintings.
A: Did you like it?
B: Not really. The paintings were strange.
A: What did you eat for dinner?
B: I ate a big pizza. It was delicious.
A: Did you get enough sleep last night?
B: No. I went to bed at 11:00.
A: Did you eat breakfast this morning?
B: No. I drank some water. I feel a bit sick.

> Where did you go yesterday?

> We went to a big art gallery.

B. Use your cards to act out Dialog 2 with a partner.

5 **Write about yourself in your notebook.**

- Where did you go last weekend?
- What did you do there?
- Did you like it?
- Did you get enough sleep last night?
- Did you eat a healthy breakfast?

All About Me

How well do I know it now?

6 **Think about it.**

A. Go to page 120. Look and circle again.

B. Check (✓).
- ☐ I can ask my teacher for help.
- ☐ I can practice.

7 **Rate this Checkpoint. Color.**

hard   OK   easy   not fun   OK   fun

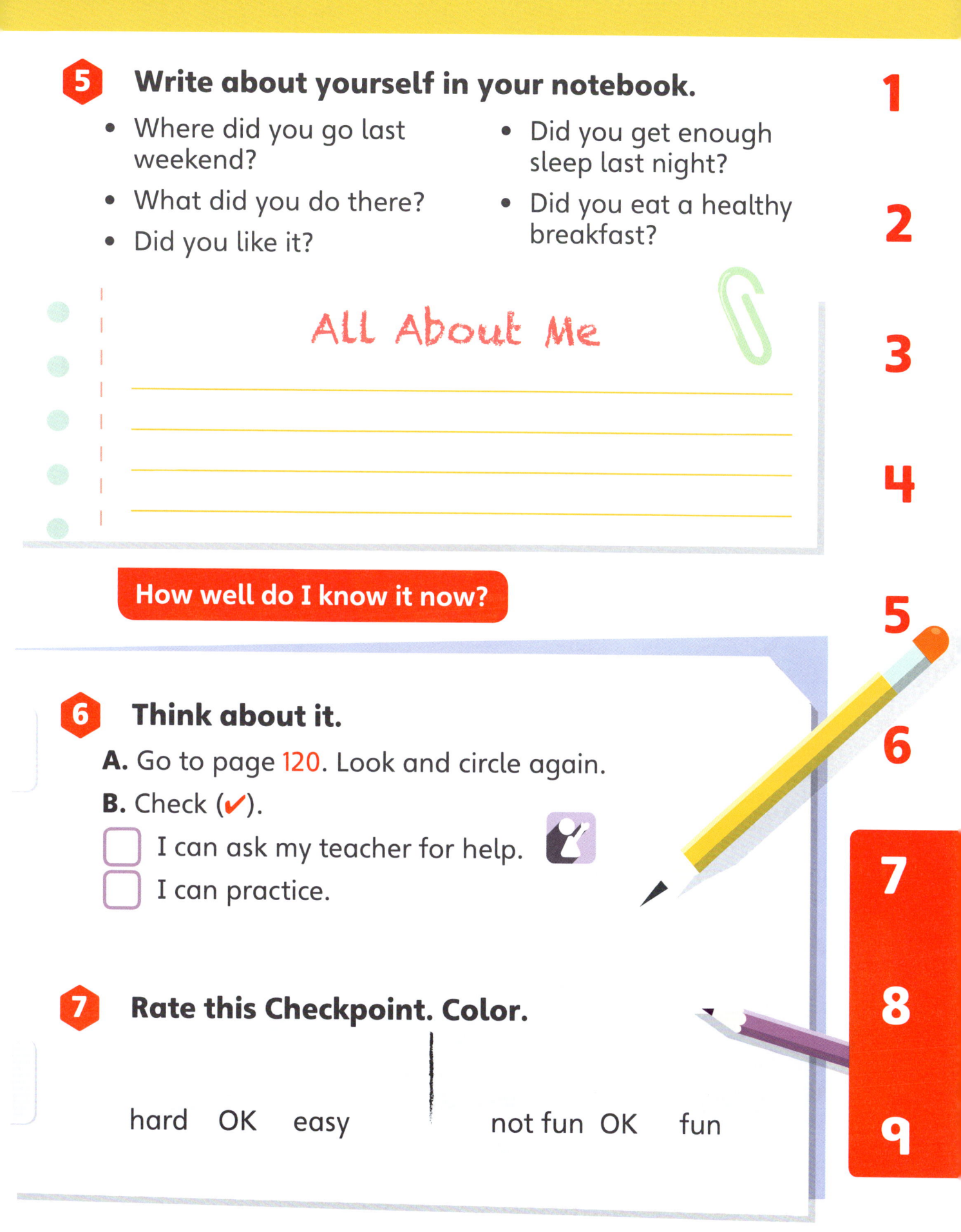

Checkpoint Units 7–9

Cambridge Young Learners English: Movers Practice Paper | Listening A

– 5 questions –

Listen and ✓ the box. There is one example.

What is his job?

A  ☐   B  ✓   C ☐

1 What is her job?

A  ☐   B  ☐   C ☐

2 What time does she usually stop working?

A  ☐   B  ☐   C ☐

124 Listening A

3 What does she have to do every day?

A ☐   B ☐   C ☐

4 What does she like about her job?

A ☐   B ☐   C ☐

5 What job would she like to have in the future?

A ☐   B ☐   C ☐

Cambridge Young Learners English: Movers Practice Paper | Listening B

– 5 questions –

Listen and draw lines. There is one example.

Mary   John   Vicky   Fred

Jack   Sally

Cambridge Young Learners English: Movers Practice Paper | Listening C

– 5 questions –

Listen and write. There is one example.

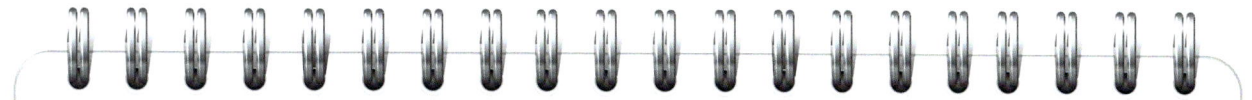

Susie's School Trip

What Susie did today: _____went on a school trip_____

1 Where she went: _____

2 What she did in the morning: _____

3 What she had for lunch: _____

4 What she did in the afternoon: _____

5 What she learned: _____

– 7 questions –

Read the story. Choose a word from the box. Write the correct word next to numbers 1–6. There is one example.

Today starts off like any other day for Paul. He ____wakes up____ and gets out of bed. Then he goes into the bathroom and ¹_____. After that, he ²_____ and takes the bus to school. But something is different today. At lunch, he doesn't have to wait in line. The other kids let him go to the front. After school, Paul comes home. He usually has to ³_____ and take him for a walk, but today his sister does it for him. In the evening, Paul's mom cooks his favorite dinner. He always has to ⁴_____ after dinner, but today he gets a break. Instead of doing chores, he gets to ⁵_____ with his brother and sister. What's different about today? It's Paul's birthday. He almost always ⁶_____ at 8 o'clock, but today his parents let him stay up late and eat ice cream. "I wish every day was like today," says Paul.

Example

My Everyday Life

My Everyday Life

My Everyday Life

My Everyday Life

My Everyday Life

My Everyday Life

My Everyday Life

My Everyday Life

My Everyday Life

7 Now choose the best name for the story.

✔ **one box.**

My Everyday Life ☐
A Very Special Day ☐
Time for a Break ☐

Reading & Writing A **129**

Cambridge Young Learners English: Movers Practice Paper | Reading & Writing B

– 5 questions –

Read the text. Choose the correct words and write them on the lines.

Example Bears live in many different kinds of places around the ___world___. Some bears live in forests and mountains. Grizzly bears, for example, live in the Rocky Mountains, in the United States. They explore when
1 the _____ is warm and they sleep during the long
2 winter. They _____ climb trees and catch fish.
3 Polar bears live in the Arctic, where it's _____
4 and cold all year round. They have thick _____ to protect them from the cold and they hunt for fish
5 under the _____. Like all other bears, they fit right into their environment.

Example ocean   desert   world

1 weather   water   world
2 can   should   will
3 snowy   hot   rainy
4 feathers   beaks   fur
5 rock   ice   wood

Cambridge Young Learners English: Movers Practice Paper | Speaking

Cutouts for Page 42, Checkpoint Units 1–3

ask a question with: **What time...**	ask a question with: **When...**	ask a question with: **in the morning / afternoon / evening**
ask a question with: **at ____:____ (time)**	ask a question with: **before work**	ask a question with: **after work**
answer with: **I...**	answer with: **I always...**	answer with: **I usually...**
answer with: **I sometimes...**	answer with: **I never...**	answer with: **I have to...**

Checkpoint Cutouts Units 1–3

Cutouts for Page 82, Checkpoint Units 4–6

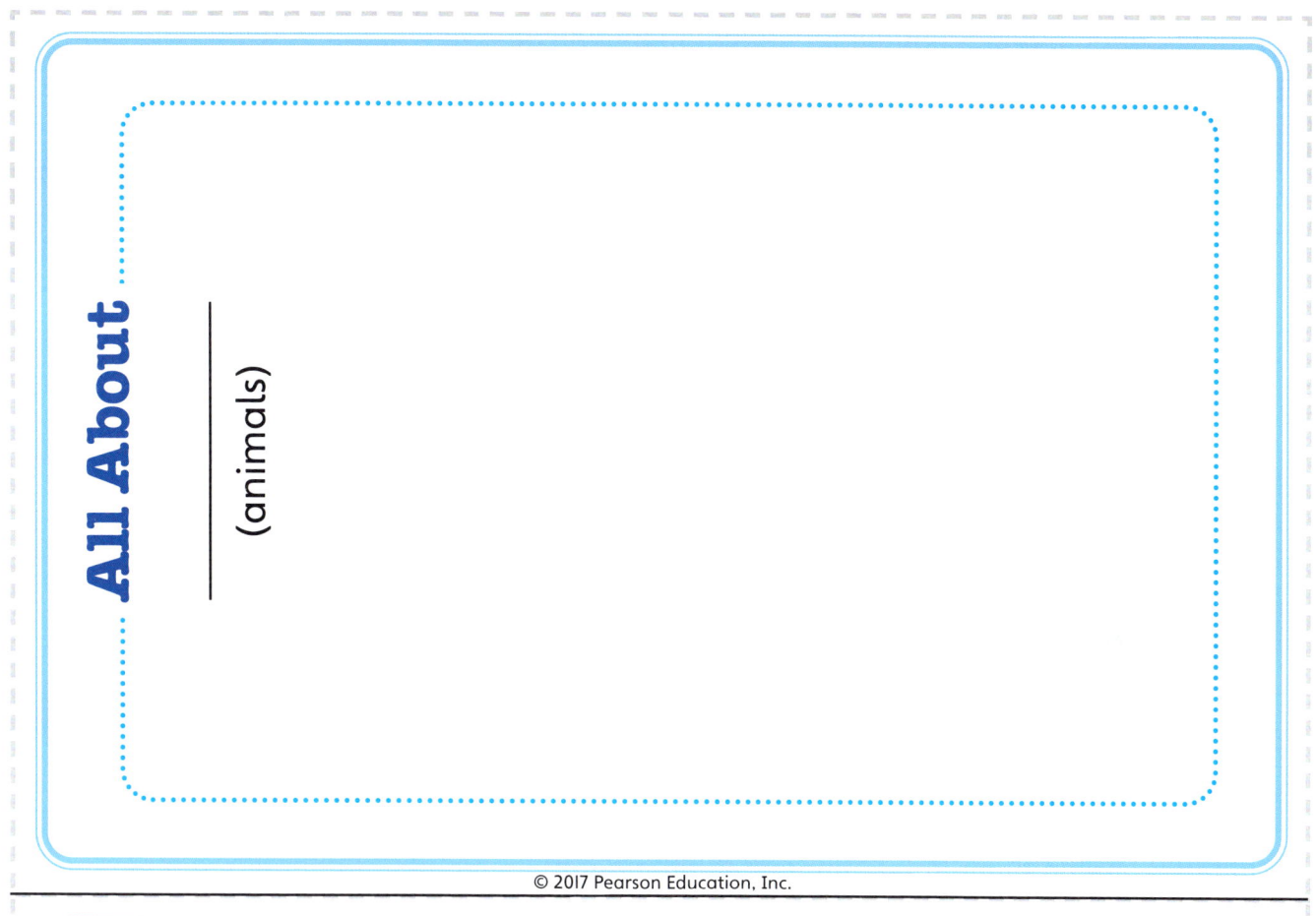

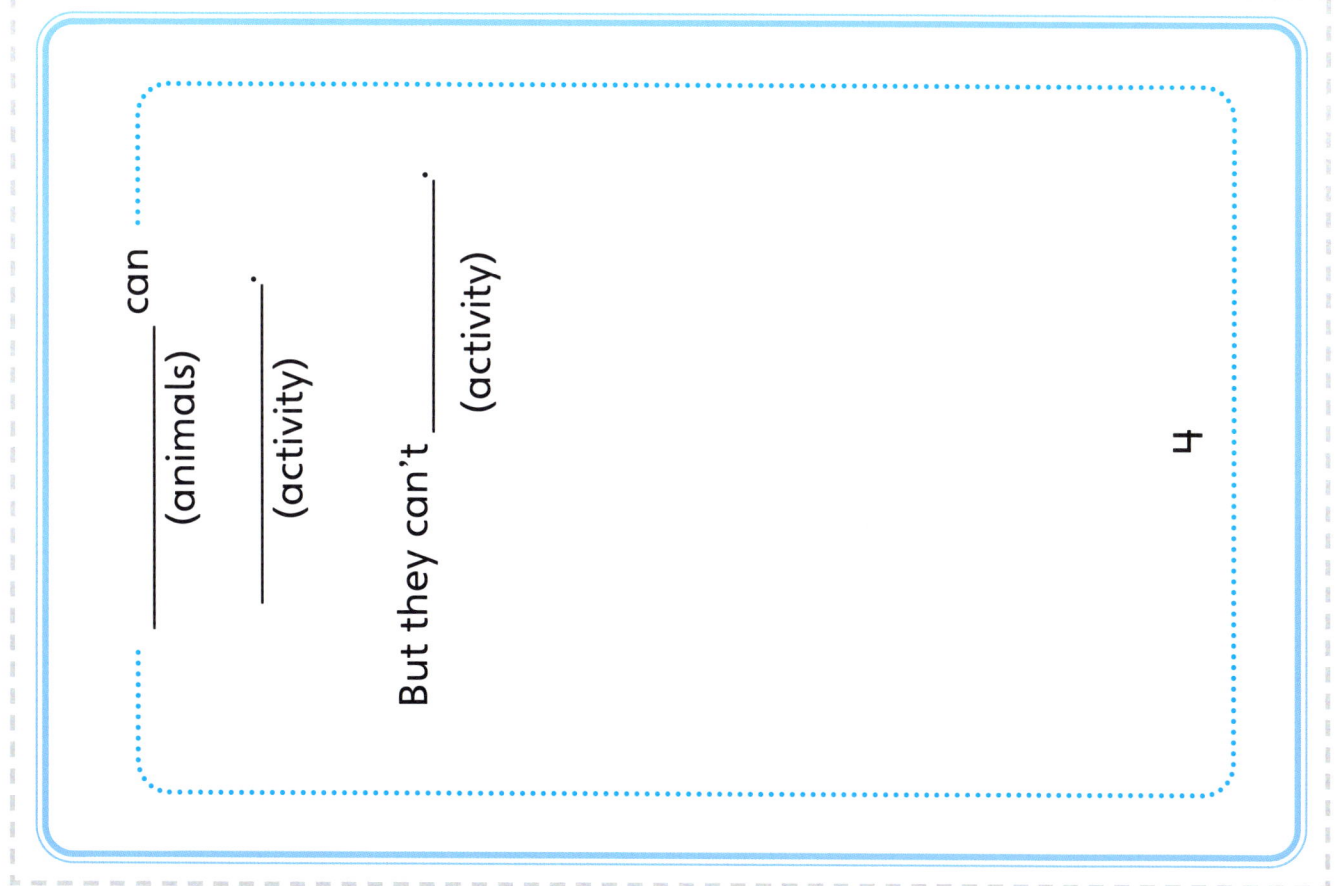

All About
_____
(animals)

_____ can
(animals)
_____.
(activity)

But they can't _____.
(activity)

4

© 2017 Pearson Education, Inc.

Checkpoint Cutouts Units 4–6 **135**

Cutouts for Page 82, Checkpoint Units 4–6

2

_____ (animals) live in _____ (habitat). It's _____ (weather word) there.

3

_____ (animals) eat _____ (food).

Cutouts for Page 122, Checkpoint Units 7–9

Dialog 2

A: Did you eat breakfast this morning?

B: Yes, it was awesome. Sharks are cool!

A: Did you like it?

B: I ate chicken, rice, and salad.

A: What did you do there?

B: Yes, I had yogurt, fruit, and toast. I'm ready for the baseball game!!

A: What did you eat for dinner?

B: We went to the aquarium.

A: Where did you go yesterday?

B: We saw a movie about sharks.

Pearson Education Limited
KAO Two
KAO Park
Harlow
Essex
CM17 9NA
England
and Associated Companies throughout the world.

www.pearsonenglish.com/bigenglish2

© Pearson Education Limited 2017

Authorised adaptation from the United States edition entitled Big English, 1st Edition, by Mario Herrera and Christopher Sol Cruz. Published by Pearson Education Inc. © 2013 by Pearson Education, Inc.

The right of Mario Herrera and Christopher Sol Cruz to be identified as the authors of this Work have been asserted by them in accordance with the Copyright, Designs and Patents Act 1988.

All rights reserved; no part of this publication may be reproduced, stored in a retrieval system, or transmitted in any form or by any means, electronic, mechanical, photocopying, recording, or otherwise without the prior written permission of the Publishers.

First published 2021

ISBN: 978-1-2923-9270-7

Set in Heinemann Roman
Printed in Slovakia by Neografia

Acknowledgements
The publisher would like to thank the following for their kind permission to reproduce photographs:
(Key: b-bottom; c-centre; l-left; r-right; t-top)

123RF.com: 89t, 89b, 91bl, 106bl, 112, 113br, belchonock 38r, Katarzyna Białasiewicz 16/10, blinztree 94 (noodles), Charles Brutlag 78br, Ihor Cherednychenko 4/9, cokemomo 94cl, Ivanka Filipova 94cr, HONGQI ZHANG 94c, Iuliia Gusakova 89c, Ivonne Wierink 10r, Brian Jackson 78bc (left), jesus David carballo prieto 51bc, Richard Martin Lee 94 (rice), Markus Mainka 91br, Nagy-Bagoly Ilona 118b, Andriy Popov 4/5, racorn 106 (b), Hans Slegers 66 (sunscreen), Sola Akindolu 72b, Olga Volodina 66 (c), waldru 78 (c), Igor Zakharevich 66 (sunglasses); **Alamy Stock Photo:** Adafim 63/2, age fotostock 94tr, allesalltag 14 (b), 28/6, Amar and Isabelle Guillen - Guillen Photo LLC 17 (f), Barry Bland 103tl, Blend Images 26r, 75bl, 88, 108/3, Brian Hickey Photography 22t, CandyBox Images 9l, 48bl, 69bl, 78cl, 95bl, 97br, 107bl, 109bl, David Grossman 61c, Design Pics 60, Directphoto Collection 16/8, Paul Doyle 17tr, Ferenc Szelepcsenyi 108/7, fStop Images GmbH 16/4, imagebroker 32t, 63/4, Interfoto 114 (a), Juniors Bildarchiv GmbH 28/8, LH Images 17 (c), Marka 108/5, MBI 8br, 32br, 33r, 45br, 48br, 73br, 78cr, 85br, 95br, 97bl, 107br, welcome cr, Nancy G Western Photography, Nancy Greifenhagen 35bl, Norbert Scanella 75br, Peter Horree 114 (b), 114 (c), Raelene Goddard 35br, Ray Evans 35tr, Ricardo Ribas 63/1, Iain Sarjeant 17 (b), Stephen French 17 (d), Tetra Images 28/1, The Picture Pantry 9ltl, Visions of America, LLC 102, Martin Wierink 84tl, William Caram 23cr, WorldFoto 108/1, ZUMA Press Inc 103b; **Digital Vision:** 44/8, 55l; **Fotolia.com:** adam121 120r, Andy Nowack 97t, Angela Köhler 62b, apops 16/7, Yuri Arcurs 16/6, Mario Beauregard 44/1, 54 (bear), bkhphoto 66 (water), Markus Bormann 29, Paul Brighton 94 (dumplings), chawalitpix 51br, chrissycopelia 78bc (right), coolmintpro 14 (c), DragonImages 22br, dule964 51tl, 54 (parrot), elnavegante 44/7, EPSTOCK 17 (a), Eric Isselée 51tr, 51cl, Michael Flippo 28/2, fothoss 56/1, galam 4/10, halayalex 69/2, 79/4, Herby (Herbert) Me 56/5, Incredible Arctic 50c, iofoto 26l, ispstock 73t, Julien Leblay 62c, karandaev 51bl, Konovalov Pavel 66 (hat), lacroix 90l, Lucky Dragon 106 (d), Malyshchyts Viktar 84/10, Michael Jell 50l, monticelllo 90r, oriori 84/2, Ornitolog82 44/5, 49, 54 (lizard), 55r, Alena Ozerova 4/1, photka 38l, Reddogs 45t, Andres Rodriguez 28/3, se media 11 (New York), Serggod 69tr, .shock 17 (e), stockphoto mania 109t, sueg0904 54 (dingo), travelwitness 17 (h), tupatu76 56/3, Valua Vitaly 11 (Montana), veneratio 44/2, vitals 84/4, 95t, vitaly tiagunov 66 (gloves), Goinyk Volodymyr 44/6, 54 (penguin), xalanx 66 (a), xamtiw 84/8; **Getty Images:** ColorBlind 14 (a), DigitalVision Vectors 11t, E+ / Juanmonino 28/4; **Pearson Education Ltd:** Jon Barlow 17tl, Gareth Boden 108/6, Trevor Clifford 5bl, 34bl, 39l, 42, Rafal Trubisz, Marcin Rosinski. Pearson Central Europe SP. Z.O.O. 100; **Shutterstock.com:** A. Einsiedler 103tr, 74c, AAR Studio 79/2, aceshot1 101t, Alvaro German Vilela 104, Andrei Kuzmik 34 (five cents), 34 (half dollar), 34 (one cent), Andrjuss 84/7, Apollofoto 9r, 20br, 21br, 24r, 61bl, 67l, 69br, 101bl, 109br, 118cr, ARENA Creative 22bl, Pierre-Yves Babelon 56/4, 64, Zaneta Baranowska 84/5, Barbara Dudzinska 91tr, bikeriderlondon 8t, 106 (c), Blend Images 23br, Brian Eichhorn 21t, Rich Carey 44/9, cellistka 54 (snake), Charles Brutlag 50r, claudia veja 20t, crshelare 44/3, Darren Baker 12, Denizo71 28/5, Diego Cervo 75tr, Jaimie Duplass 57, 66 (b), 80, dwphotos 115t, Eric Isselee 54 (koala), 74t, fenghui 17 (g), Fotokostic 118tl, Xavier Gallego Morell 72t, Gelpi JM 69/3, Goodluz 16/5, greenland 28/7, Guitar photographer 63/3, gvictoria 5br, 20bl, 21bl, 24l, 32bl, 33l, 45bl, 61br, 67r, 82, 85bl, 106br, hartphotography 5t, 40, Mat Hayward 69tl, hlphoto 91c, holbox 78 (b), HomeArt 115c, idiz 54 (kangaroo), iko 69/5, Ivaschenko Roman 84/6, Matthew Jacques 108/2, John Roman Images 16/3, K2 PhotoStudio 4/2, kamonrat 52, Karina Bakalyan 84/9, kccullenPhoto 94tl, Kokhanchikov 69/4, 79/1, Kotenko Oleksandr 56/2, Gareth Leung 54 (kookaburra), Lisa F. Young 11 (Texas), 16/1, 36b, Ljupco Smokovski 75tl, Lotus_studio 5lcr, Petr Malyshev 66 (umbrella), MaraZe 84/3, Mau Horng 10c, 92t, michaeljung 16/9, Stuart Miles 4/4, Monkey Business Images 48t, 107t, 118tc, Nadezda Zavitaeva 115b, NaughtyNut 23tl, Dmitry Naumov 106 (a), P A 35tl, Phil MacD Photography 108/4, Philoul000 35c, PhotoBarmaley 61t, Photocreo Michal Bednarek 23bl, PixieMe 4/3, Preto Perola 84/1 (bread), Rob Marmion 4/6, 11 (California), Rus S 79/3, Sergey Toronto 62t, shupian 78 (a), sianc 78bl, Smileus 10l, Sniegirova Mariia 69tc, Solphoto 69/1, Stacy Barnett 23cl, David Steele 44/4, stefanolunardi 4/8, James Steidl 118tr, Steve Wood 34 (one dollar), Susan Schmitz 79t, Lyudmila Suvorova 84br, Syda Productions 20c, The_Sangkhung 23tr, Christy Thompson 16/2, tobkatrina 36t, Tom Reichner 74b, tororo reaction 108/8, 120c, Ultrashock 54 (mountain lion), Valentyn Volkov 92b, wavebreakmedia 4/7, 79/5, yadom 113t, yalayama 8bl, 34br, 39r, 73bl, 101br, 113bl, 118cl, 119, welcome cl; **SuperStock:** Blend Images 85t, 120l

Cover images: Front: **Alamy Stock Photo:** RooM the Agency

All other images © Pearson Education

Every effort has been made to trace the copyright holders and we apologise in advance for any unintentional omissions. We would be pleased to insert the appropriate acknowledgement in any subsequent edition of this publication.

Illustrated by
Tiago Americo, Martyn Cain, Andrew Hennessey, Sean@KJA-Artists, Victor Moshpoulos, Zaharias Papadopoulos, Remy Simard, Christos Skaltsas